DOG DAYS

'I've got a sociologist called Nuzek coming in this afternoon with his latest book. On *Protestantism and Pornography*.'

Faced with such a prospect, Peter, the protagonist of Simon Gray's new play, finds the idea of sitting at his desk in a publishing house considerably less attractive than attempting to seduce a free-lance cover designer while his wife is out teaching English to foreigners and shopping at Sainsbury's. *Dog Days* is about the sad and hilarious consequences of Peter's disenchantment with his job, his wife, his public school master brother and himself.

The play is a companion piece to Simon Gray's enormously successful *Otherwise Engaged* and has the same remarkable blend of wit and pathos, humour and despair. It is scheduled for a first production at the Oxford Playhouse in October 1976.

The photograph of Simon Gray on the back cover is reproduced by courtesy of Beryl Gray.

Simon Gray

DOG DAYS

EYRE METHUEN · LONDON

First published in 1976 by Eyre Methuen Ltd
11 New Fetter Lane, London EC4P 4EE
Copyright © 1976 by Simon Gray
Typeset by TNR Publications Ltd,
11 Greek Street, London W1V 5LE
Printed in Great Britain
by Cox & Wyman Ltd, Fakenham, Norfolk

ISBN 0 413 37260 X (Hardback)
ISBN 0 413 37270 7 (Paperback)

Author's Note

Dog Days was begun before the final draft of another play—
Butley—was in production, was continued at odd moments
during rehearsals and completed—frequently and variously—
during the next two years or so. It was just one of a number of
plays I was working on in an increasing state of muddle that
was eventually like a madness. There were moments when,
nauseated into lucidity by the piles of typescript that filled my
drawers, my cupboard, an antique chest and two pinewood
coffins, I swore I'd never write again; which I would have to
amend, as I crouched a few minutes later at my typewriter,
into the more calming proposition that I would merely never
finish anything again.

So I went on and on, covering page after page. Characters
from one play would slip into another, change name, age,
occupation and even sex, before either slipping into yet another
play or back into the first. The same passages of dialogue
cropped up in different scenes, in different plays, sometimes in
different scenes in the same play or plays. At the end of each
session I squirrelled the newly-written pages away for
tomorrow or next week; for whenever I might be short. I was
the Casaubon of show business.

I doubt if I could ever have stopped, if I hadn't had to go to
New York. In the ten days before my departure I wrote an
entirely new and above all freshly conceived piece that probably
differed only in the odd passage here and there from its first
version, dropped it off at my agent's on the way to the airport,
and left him to decide whether to pass it to a producer or return

it to me. Both agent and producer cabled me in New York. I remember settling into an armchair in the lobby of the Algonquin and toasting their adjectives—routinely intoxicating—in champagne, before going on to glare, several stages later and through a brandy fog, at their noun; which was 'draft'. As its implications became increasingly distinct, so did my future as a writer. I would never finish anything again. I would never write anything again.

Back in London I was given lunch with my agent by the producer in an expensive Spanish restaurant (a good omen, but not conclusive; an invitation to the Cafe Royal would, in a sense, have made the lunch unnecessary). A copy of *Dog Days,* that the producer had had re-typed and bound (also a good omen) lay between us as we pursued the preliminary courtesies that always run, in these situations, from the first hand-shake through to coffee. They had both read the play again ('several times', but that was a metaphor) and were prepared to add a few more adjectives to their cabled lists. It seemed to them too, to be far less of a 'draft' than they had first thought it. 'It was all there.' So much so, in fact, that we must think about a director, and could certainly talk about casting, dates, venues, etc. But perhaps a director first, with whom I could collaborate —'if I were too close to the script to face it alone'—on whatever needed doing. What needed doing? Oh, a little work, no more—a revision in the second scene of the first act, did I think? the mildest of personality changes to the central character (a dash of motivation, perhaps)—and well, a touch of economy and a modicum of expansion—in different places, of course. Certainly nothing more than most plays needed in rehearsal anyway, for, after all, it was from 75 to 95 per cent *all there.* Good.

I took the producer's copy with me when I left—that night I threw it, along with everything I'd written in the two years since *Butley,* out with the other rubbish. Some day I might begin again. But not in my lifetime, as I saw it. At least, I hoped not.

It was extraordinary to be free. In my study now only the usual bottles, books; empty drawers and chests; a clear desk; a typewriter which could at last be put to proper use (abusive letters to friends, relatives and other strangers, for instance). It was as if I had rid myself of an aged and incontinent alter ego. Halved back to my only self, I could keep things clean.

My agent sent me his copy of *Dog Days*. I tossed it unopened into a chest. The Director of the Palace Theatre, Watford, telephoned to arrange a lunch. Over it he reminded me that I owed him a play. It had been promised years before, but he'd tactfully held back until I had nothing left to give. We went to my house and into my study and opened the chest. We met shortly afterwards to arrange a production.

Within two or three months I'd finished two television plays—*Plaintiffs and Defendants* and *Two Sundays*—and a stage play, *Otherwise Engaged*. It is possible that these three pieces evolved out of the unrelated labour that preceded them, but it is far more likely that I embarrassed myself into them at the prospect of *Dog Days* being performed.

My agent sent the two television plays to the BBC, and I hurried *Otherwise Engaged* off to Watford. But the Director of its Palace Theatre was by this time passionately committed to *Dog Days*, and would accept no substitute. So *Otherwise Engaged* went to the producer who had talked of doing *Dog Days*, and the Director of the Palace Theatre, Watford, generously agreed to postpone his production until the year after *Otherwise Engaged* had opened in London.

December 1975

Post script. It was not, after all, to be so easy. I went on behaving badly towards the Watford Palace Theatre and its director during the year that followed the opening of *Otherwise Engaged*, pleading that I wasn't yet up to discussions about a production of another play, with all the concentration it demanded and all the prospects (of casting, rehearsals, etc) it opened out, until he became increasingly cynical about my intentions (while remaining admirably a friend) and went off to the States on a year's visiting scholarship. And that was that. Until some time later a sudden show of interest from the Oxford Playhouse revived my own interest. I agreed to do it there, and to direct it myself. The by now habitual reaction followed. Almost at once I dispatched a grovelling message through my agent withdrawing the piece. One of the Playhouse directors came down to London to see me, we talked over lunch, and at its conclusion I agreed to restore the play to him, with the understanding that I shouldn't direct it myself (after such a display of doubt how could I?) and that I shouldn't again change my mind. I shan't. *Dog Days* will open at the Oxford Playhouse in October, 1976 — God and the other devils willing; and I shall find out for myself at last what it is precisely I've been dreading all this time.

August 1976

DOG DAYS

DOG DAYS was first presented at the
Oxford Playhouse on 26 October 1976
with the following cast:

PETER   Charles Kay
CHARLES   Richard Wilson
HILARY   Gayle Hunnicutt
JOANNA   Emma Williams

Directed by Gordon McDougall
Set designed by Saul Radomsky
Lighting by David Colmer

Act One

Scene One

JOANNA enters from the kitchen, tentatively. She has a folio under her arm. She puts it down on the table, sees the photograph, looks at it.

PETER. *(Enters from the kitchen, carrying two mugs of Nescafé).* Only instant, I'm afraid. The trick is to pretend it's not coffee at all, but a quite other beverage. *(Takes a sip of his own)* The next trick is to like the other beverage.

JOANNA. Oh this is great. I was just looking—*(Puts the picture down)* Are they your parents?

PETER. Yes, in our old garden in Bromley.

JOANNA. Your Dad's a fine figure of a man, I love his balaclava, is it from the war or something?

PETER. Actually that's my mother in her gardening gear. But you're right, she was a fine figure of a man. That's my father there, on the edge of the picture as usual. In the fine figure of the little husband.

JOANNA. He's got a really nice smile.

PETER. Hasn't he? A positive advertisement.

JOANNA. For what, your mother you mean?

PETER. No, drunkenness.

JOANNA. Oh. Did he drink too much then?

PETER. He did, yes.

JOANNA. But he gave it up?

PETER. Oh, nothing so drastic. He got killed in a car crash some years ago.

JOANNA. Oh God, I'm sorry. How terrible.

PETER. For whom?

JOANNA. Well, your mother . . .

PETER. Not at all.

JOANNA. You mean she didn't mind?

PETER. She didn't have time to, as she was driving. She always insisted they do everything together, you see. Except drink. And sleep. That's me on his shoulders, by the way.

JOANNA. Oh. Oh yes. And who's this between your mother's legs?

PETER. My brother Charlie. He used to lurk there until quite late in life. He's something of a home body. He's got lots of children of his own now.

JOANNA. Really, how many?

PETER. Actually, I'm never quite sure, but it works on an opposite system to one's bank account. More than one remembered. He's half Catholic.

JOANNA. *Half* Catholic?

PETER. His wife is, and he's wholly married.

JOANNA. You're not married, though?

PETER. Certainly not. Charlie's done enough for two.

JOANNA. Then you have this place all to yourself?

PETER. Well, we're not allowed upstairs.

JOANNA. Who?

PETER. You and I.

JOANNA. Oh. Who lives there?

PETER. My landlady.

JOANNA. Is she in now?

PETER. No, she works. She teaches English to foreigners at one of those dingy academies off Oxford Street. Then she picks up her little boy from school. She's never back until four-thirty to five on Wednesdays, she has to do some shopping at Sainsbury's. So they won't disturb us.

JOANNA. Is *she* married?

PETER. Yes, she is.

JOANNA. What's he like?

PETER. Like any other landlord in the Muswell Hill area. He goes down as his property value goes up.

JOANNA. Down where?

PETER. Downhill. All the way to Islington, if he can make it. *(Puts his mug down, turns away.)*

JOANNA. I'm sorry, I always ask questions when I'm nervous. You're the first editor I've shown my work to, and I've been puffing myself up so much that now you're going to look at it I keep putting off the big moment. Well—*(Opens the folio, shows him).* I know it's not your department, you do all the intellectual stuff I know, but I'd really value your opinion.

PETER. Ah, nudes. I like nudes. The one on the left though, the chap's a bit fat isn't he—oh, they're both chaps.

JOANNA. Well yes.

PETER. What's it for, a homosexual sex manual, nobody told *me* we were doing one.

JOANNA. No, it's that dieting manual. Those blokes are before and after.

PETER. I see. Before looks altogether nicer, I like that.

JOANNA. Do you think you people will go on using me, now you've started?

PETER. Oh once we people start using people, we never stop. In life, as in art. *(Goes over, grabs her, kisses her clumsily.)*

JOANNA. *(struggles free).* Hey, you haven't even looked at it properly.

PETER. Well, I'm a little short of time.

JOANNA.   Time for what? *(Pause).* Oh, I get it, bed you mean?

PETER. It'll have to be the sofa actually. But if we take the slip-cover off and plump up the pillows it'll pass muster. *(Pause).* Well, the wooing *is* going on rather, isn't it, like one of those hors d'oeuvres that stop you getting to the main course. *(Pause).* And I've got a sociologist called Nuzek coming in this afternoon with his latest book. On *Protestantism and Pornography.* I'll see if I can't get you the dust-jacket. *(Comes over to her, takes her in his arms again, kisses her.)* Something on the lines of that one would do very well—the thin nude could be Protestantism and the fat one Pornography, or the other way around even. I could get you lots more commissions—*(Kisses her)*.

JOANNA. Get off me! *(Forces him away)*. What sort of fool do you think I am?

PETER. My sort, I hope . . .

JOANNA. You're married!

PETER. Good God, who to?

JOANNA. That landlady of yours.

PETER. Scarcely.

JOANNA. Scarcely what?

PETER. Scarcely eight years.

JOANNA. And that little boy's your son. Well, isn't he?

PETER. If I answer that question with too much confidence, I'll destroy the premise of a whole tragic literature. Besides, he's *very* little, if you stare straight ahead you won't even see him. *(Moves towards JOANNA again)*.

JOANNA. *(Moves away)*. I don't sleep with married men, I'm afraid.

PETER. Of what? We're very well trained.

JOANNA. Jesus, what a prick!

PETER. *(angrily)*. What a *what?*

JOANNA. Prick, that's what you are, a prick!

PETER. Oh, thank God, I thought you said *prig*.

JOANNA. Is this the way out too? *(Gestures towards kitchen, right)*.

PETER. Right into the boulevards of Muswell Hill. I'll go this way *(gestures to the left),* and wink at the neighbours.

JOANNA. And in your own home too. *(Turns, goes out with portfolio).*

PETER. *(stands for a moment, then goes to the window, leans out).* Hey—hey—what about *your* place then?

Waits, gets no response, turns, goes to the drinks table, pours himself a stiff scotch, adds soda water, swallows it down, looks at his wrist watch, picks up his brief-case. Goes out, left.

Lights down.

Lights up.

The room full of sunlight. Outside the sound of children's voices at play. Toys and Sunday bits and pieces scattered around the room. After a moment, PETER enters, left, in weekend wear and very sloppy. He is smoking. He looks towards the window, winces, goes to the drinks table, pours himself a scotch, squirts in soda water, turns, goes to the sofa.

CHARLES. *(off, outside the window, right).* Nindy, what a clever girlie, did you do this just for Daddy, thank you darling, thank you. Now you go and watch the big ones play football while Daddy takes this in and looks for Uncle Peter.

PETER listens to this, then turns over on the sofa, cupping his cigarette and drink.

CHARLES enters, carrying a plastic pot. He goes through and out, left. He's also in weekend wear, but neat, short-haired and springy of step.

PETER adjusts himself more comfortably, sips from his drink, puffs on his cigarette.

Sound of tap running, lavatory flushing, left.

PETER takes up his defensive position, back to the audience.

CHARLES re-enters, left, carrying the pot. He hesitates, goes to the drinks table, then puts the pot down on it as he squirts himself an enormous soda water. Begins to drain it off, becomes aware that somebody is on the sofa. Goes over, looks down at PETER.

CHARLES. Pete!

PETER. *(rolls over).* Hi Charlie.

CHARLES. What on earth are you doing?

PETER. Practising.

CHARLES. Practising what?

PETER. Secret drinking.

CHARLES. Oh, I see. Not feeling very sociable, eh?

PETER. On the contrary, but it's such a rare feeling I like to savour it on my own. *(Gets up, goes to the window).*

CHARLES. *(watches him).* I must say, you've been acting very strangely today. We've scarcely seen you, except at lunch. Is something the matter?

PETER. No.

CHARLES. Frankly some of your remarks were a bit off.

PETER. Really? *(Staring out of the window).* Probably because I've kept them in too long. Did you know that Alison's joined the boys in football. Is that wise at seven months gone? I should warn you that Jeremy's got a powerful shot for a five year old *and* has a nasty English habit of going over the top.

CHARLES. Oh, she'll be all right, you know how active she is during her pregnancies. Peter . . .

PETER. And between them too, to get to them so quickly. When do you intend to stop exactly? I realise Alison's a practising Catholic but this'll make six in five years . . .

CHARLES. Four, actually. In six years. As I'm sure *you* realise. And you also realise, because I've told you often enough, that we *both* happen to believe in letting them come as they please.

PETER. Well, you certainly do please them, from the speed at which they keep coming.

CHARLES. The important thing is that they please *us.* Anyway, now that you've chosen to raise the subject, Alison and I sometimes wonder what you two have got against having more.

PETER. Contraceptives, and they work miracles.

CHARLES. Oh ha ha. But has it ever occurred to you that it might turn out a little hard on Jeremy himself? He'll be the one that'll have to cope with being an only child.

PETER. If I can cope with being an only father, when we need two or three, he can cope with being an only child when we don't need any more.

CHARLES. Something's the matter, isn't it?

PETER. With what?

CHARLES. With you. For one thing you're smoking and drinking far more than usual.

PETER. Oh that's quite usual with smoking and drinking.

CHARLES. But Pete, think of your health! I'm sure you would feel much better if you cut down.

PETER. Ah, but then I wouldn't have the scotch and fags I need to help me endure it.

CHARLES. Endure what?

PETER. My health. *(Toasts himself)*. I notice you've cut down though. To the very bottom. And the last time you were here you'd fought your way up to five a day wasn't it?

CHARLES. Only because I was under some stress.

PETER. What stress?

CHARLES. I was still waiting to hear whether I'd got it.

PETER. Got what?

CHARLES. The assistant Headmastership at Ampleside.

PETER. And did you?

CHARLES. Not only did Alison phone Hilary as soon as I'd phoned her, but before lunch today Alison actually described a sort of informal interview she'd had with Headmaster.

PETER. Oh, that was with Headmaster!

CHARLES. Who did you think it was with?

PETER. Her gynaecologist.

CHARLES. *That* was during lunch.

PETER. She had an interview with her gynaecologist during lunch . . .

CHARLES. Oh ha ha.

PETER. Well, anyway Charlie, congratulations. I know how much you respect that Headmaster of yours. It'll be wonderful to work so closely with him, won't it?

CHARLES. Yes, it will.

PETER. He's a great influence over your life, isn't he?

CHARLES. In some things, perhaps, I don't deny it.

PETER. How can you, when there's scarcely a decision, large or small, on which you don't consult him—where he leads, you follow, eh?

CHARLES. I wouldn't go that far.

PETER. Really? How far has he gone?

CHARLES. It's no good, you won't get at me through Headmaster, you know.

PETER. Does he smoke?

CHARLES. He's got far too much sense.

PETER. Does he drink?

CHARLES. Yes, he does.

PETER. What does he drink?

CHARLES. The odd wine, why?

PETER. That wine you brought along for lunch was odd, was it one of his?

CHARLES. It was a retzina.

PETER. Home-made though, wasn't it?

CHARLES. How on earth would one make retzina?

PETER. Exactly as the Greeks do, I should think. By boiling up some tree bark.

CHARLES. Didn't you make it clear enough at lunch what you thought of it—sniffing at your glass and making faces to yourself? I got the message, Pete!

PETER. You've got that smirk on, Charlie.

CHARLES. *What* smirk?

PETER. Your lying smirk.

CHARLES. Lying—what lie, for Heaven's sake! *(Little pause).* I never said it wasn't home-made, I just wanted to make sure you really guessed. I had a little bet with Alison when we decanted it into that bottle that you wouldn't. Which I'm now perfectly prepared to admit I lose, all right!

PETER. Who gave you the recipe?

CHARLES. It's a traditional one from Cyprus, that's been handed down.

PETER. To whom? Headmaster?

CHARLES. His wife, actually. Now I really think I ought to go out and help Alison and Hilary entertain the children—are you coming, or are you going to stay here?

PETER. They're vegetarian too, aren't they, Headmaster and wife?

CHARLES. Yes they are, *so what?*

PETER. And that's why you and Alison have given up meat, is it?

CHARLES. Given up meat? Didn't you see me put Hilary's casserole away?

PETER. Yes, into your handkerchief. You used to employ the same technique with Mummy's Friday night fish stews—until she asked you to explain why your trouser pockets smelt of haddock.

CHARLES. *(after a long pause).* Yes, well I do apologise for that. The truth is, as we'd forgotten to warn Hilary, and as we realised she'd gone to a lot of trouble to cook for us, we felt it a matter of common courtesy to go through with it. Frankly, we knew the children would more than make up for us. *(Little pause).* I do hope she didn't notice, though.

PETER. Oh, you were as skilful as ever. The funny smile, the elaborate chewing, the dabs at your lips. You may have made her casserole look inedible, but you did look as if you were managing to eat it. Is it still in your pocket?

CHARLES. Yes.

PETER. Well, you can chuck it into the garbage now, I won't sneak.

CHARLES. Actually, I'd rather keep it.

PETER. Keep it!

CHARLES. Yes.

PETER. In your pocket?

CHARLES. For the time being.

PETER. *(after a pause).* Oh I see, no cloistered

and fugitive virtue for you, eh Charlie? You like to carry your vice around with you, to fight every moment of the day. A handkerchief full of temptation!—I just hope you don't spill it out in front of Headmaster when you have to blow your nose. He mightn't believe your story.

CHARLES. *(slowly).* Ha. Ha. Ha. I happen to want it for a dog.

PETER. You haven't got a dog.

CHARLES. No, but the school has. Alfonso—at least that's what I call him. He's a sort of stray that's always in and out of Headmaster's garden. Somebody's got to feed him.

PETER. And you've chosen my wife? Why can't Headmaster do the job, it's his garden. Or doesn't he like animals.

CHARLES. I'm sure he loves them. And I *know* his wife does. So I expect they do feed him. But I also expect he'd be grateful for any little tid-bits. Does that clear that up? There can't be any further questions Pete— now that you've managed to embarrass me, after all.

PETER. Well, just one.

CHARLES. I don't think I want to hear it.

PETER. OK. *(Goes and stands by the window).*

CHARLES. *(Stands uncertainly, then goes to the soda water, takes a swift draught from his glass, looks at PETER).* All right, what is it?

PETER. Mmmmm?

CHARLES. Your last question?

PETER. Mmm. Oh yes—Did you give up meat, cigarettes

and alcohol—except for boiled tree bark, that is—*before* your appointment as Assistant, to·ingratiate yourself with Headmaster? Or *afterwards,* on his orders? Or did you do it *during* the interview, in a series of dramatic renunciations?

CHARLES. I didn't give up, or have to give up, anything to get the Assistantship. Alison and I merely observed how well Headmaster and his wife looked on their regimen and drew a sane conclusion which would doubtless have escaped you. Furthermore, far from feeling ashamed of it, I don't mind telling you that I, personally, feel absolutely marvellous for it. As if I were fifteen again!

PETER. I'm sorry to hear that. You were particularly ghastly at fifteen. Even Mummy thought so.

CHARLES. At least *I* see the world properly, in its vivid details. And most of what I see, I like. What do *you* see at the moment, Pete?

PETER. Nothing much to like, I admit, Charlie. *(Little pause).* Actually, from my recollection of Alison's gynaecological anecdotes, delivered during the lunch she was presumably pocketing in her pregnancy trousers, you don't have to give up anything to get the vivid details. As long, that is, as you don't give up Alison.

CHARLES. Right! That does it! I spent the whole morning trying to overlook your bloody nasty remarks—

PETER. Spoilsport.

CHARLES. But don't worry, I'm not going to overlook that one. You jeer at my feeling fifteen, but you must have gone right back to the nursery to insult my wife like that.

PETER. You didn't have a wife like that in the nursery, Charlie. Or are you about to spring into the Freudian open by naming Mummy? Come to think of it we didn't have a nursery either. We were allowed the run of a box-room in a semi-detached in Bromley which *she* called a nursery for the same reason that she used to call that ghastly institution she made the drunken mouse buy us into, a public school.

CHARLES. Wundale is a Public School! *(Pause)*. *What* did you say about Mummy? *(Pause)*. And Daddy?

PETER. That you're fulfilling her ambitions to the hilt, Charlie. And I can't say worse than that, can I? You may have risen a notch in greasing your way into the Assistant Headmastership at Amplesides, but then she got you to plan *your* public school early, didn't she, in the Wundale Remove at thirteen. And you don't intend to stop until you get all the way to Eton in your mid-forties, when you'll be the first real old, or at least middle-aged, public school boy in the family.

CHARLES. Why, you little—*(Makes as if to hit PETER, checks himself)*. *You* have the nerve to talk about snobs —a man whose sole ambition was to end up editing books he's discovered too late he despises and so is stuck as a Junior Editor — and for life, the way you're going on. And quite rightly given your attitude. A muddled little Oxford pseud, whose only way of elevating himself is to sneer at other people. I'd hoped you'd grown up a little since marrying Hilary, but you haven't have you? That's what you've really reverted to, isn't it—a cheap little undergraduate.

PETER. Not at all cheap. I cost the State quite a lot of money.

CHARLES. You little—*(Pulls himself together, and with dignity).* If it weren't for Hilary's feelings, and Jeremy's—I wouldn't set foot in this house again. *(Turns, goes towards exit kitchen, right).*

PETER. That's where a graduate of Oxford and a graduate of Reading have more in common than either of us thought, Charlie. Because those are my own sentiments exactly. *(As CHARLES, unhearing, exits, collapses on sofa).*

There is a lighting change, to suggest time passing. PETER *lights a cigarette. Much activity from the kitchen, right.*

HILARY. *(Enters. Looks at* PETER, *and as she begins to clear up toys and bits and pieces).* Jeremy is in bed, I trust.

PETER. *(not stirring).* Yup.

HILARY. And did you bother to get him to read to you?

PETER. Until we both realised he still couldn't.

HILARY. Of course he can.

PETER. Then we have a wonderchild who can read with his eyes shut. My own view is that he was reciting.

HILARY. You probably made him nervous.

PETER. Not as nervous as he made me. 'This is Janet. This is John. That is Janet. That is John.' *(In a singsong).* I thought he was trying to put me under a spell. I was reading at four. So were you. So was everybody in our day, except Charlie, and he made it by five and a half.

HILARY. And except those who'd never read. Because they were never taught.

PETER. Oh, I recognise the modern system is more democratic. Now everybody gets taught but nobody reads.

HILARY. What would *you* know about the modern system, as you don't even go to the lectures the school lays on to explain it.

PETER. I went to the first, if you remember; in which case you'll also remember that it was doubtful whether the lady who gave the lecture could read, she could scarcely talk. But don't worry darling, it's all being attended to. We publishers are working hand in hand with the Department of Education. They're making it their job to ensure that our Jeremy won't read when he grows up, and we're making it ours to ensure that if he grows up there are no books around worth his reading. I promise you our son shall not feel deprived! What's left can be read by those foreigners you teach, most of whom seem to be writing them anyway, judging by the standard of the English I'm called on to edit.

HILARY has gone to the door, toys etc in her arms. Turns, glares at him.

By God, I believe that's what's known as a level look, or would be if it weren't for your slight squint, now you're tired.

HILARY. *(Sees the pot, manages to pick it up.)* Do you mean you've just lolled there, letting it stare you in the face?

PETER. I did try staring back, but it remained unmoved.

HILARY. Could you at least open the door, please!

PETER gets up, saunters over, opens the door, swivelling at the same time to pick up the scotch. As HILARY exits, pours himself a glass, lights a cigarette. Goes back to sofa, after a pause.

HILARY off, calls something.

PETER. Wah—?

HILARY calls again.

Right, fine, fine. *(Goes back to the sofa, settles onto it.)*

HILARY. *(Enters, stage left.)* God, I wish you'd at least answer me when I call.

PETER. I did.

HILARY. And what did you say?

PETER. Wah—? Right, fine and fine.

HILARY. And what sort of answer is that?

PETER. What sort of question was it?

HILARY. That typescript that's been lying in the lavatory since Thursday, how important is it?

PETER. To Nuzek, the Polish socio-prophet, very. Because he wrote it. To me, not at all. I'm merely its editor.

HILARY. So you won't have to read it then?

PETER. Nobody who buys it will read it, why should I?

HILARY. And those reviewers you used to worry about so—won't they notice if it's not edited?

PETER. Oh, they can write their reviews from my blurb.

HILARY. And what will you write your blurb from?

PETER. Their last reviews. It's what's known in publishing as a benign circle. Nuzek's reputation depends on nobody reading him. His prose guarantees that nobody will. You're taking an unusual interest in the mysteries of my little trade, darling, how come?

HILARY. Only to find whether wha—? right, fine and fine were reasonable answers to my question. *(Goes over to the desk, picks up a brief-case beside it, takes out some papers.)*

PETER. And how did I do?

HILARY. All right, it appears. *(Beginning to sort through.)* As it clearly doesn't matter that either Jeremy or one of your nephews blocked the lavatory with it this afternoon.

PETER. Christ, they didn't!

HILARY. I thought you said it didn't matter.

PETER. But he's coming to our six simultaneous publications party in a couple of weeks. He could ruin it if he finds out about this. We've already asked the Brendan Behan of Women's Lib along to do the swearing and fighting. Ah well, I'll just have to tell him our son mistook it for a bottom copy. *(Gets up, goes to the drinks table.)* Drink?

HILARY. No thanks.

PETER. *(Pouring himself a large one, adding soda water).* Ah, I've been looking forward to this all day.

HILARY. Really? What's so special about the fifth or sixth?

PETER. It's backed up by four or five others. By the way, how do you think your casserole went down with Charlie and Alison? *(Sitting down again)*.

HILARY. You needn't bother.

PETER. What?

HILARY. Alison confessed in the garden.

PETER. Oh. *(Little pause)* In the garden she confessed, did she? She really does practise away at her Catholicism, in Church, in the open air, in bed—I must say, she's pretty swollen, even for nine months swollen older Alison. Do you think that gynaecologist of hers has taught her how to begin the next before delivering the last? She surely doesn't bother with such fripperies as labour any more—just a brief muscular spasm something like a hiccough. Oh, I remember when she was a mere slip of a lump of a thing—studying Charlie and English at Reading, who would have believed—Why even prophetic Nuzek will be a mite perplexed to hear—that because my brother happened to marry a lump of a slip whose reproductive organs might have been plumbed by the Vatican itself, his *Protestantism and Pornography* is currently washing through the sewers of London . . .

HILARY has got together her papers, and is on her way out.

What about some supper, I'm peckish. *(Taking her by the wrist.)*

HILARY. Are you? Then you'll have to get it yourself.

PETER. Why?

HILARY. Because I've got to finish these tonight.

PETER. Why?

HILARY. So that I can brush up on some phonetics to-morrow before taking Jeremy to school.

PETER. Why? Is his classless accent slipping?

HILARY. Unless of course you take him for once. Can you?

PETER. Darling, I don't drive, remember. You do.

HILARY. It's within walking distance. He could easily manage it.

PETER. But I couldn't. Besides, he'd use up my whole day's supply of artless prattle, which I'm going to need for my work. (*Little pause.*) Surely even in these glum days a wife can rustle up a sandwich and cocoa for hubby, before hurrying off to her diversions.

HILARY. Diversions! My diversions! Do you mean these! *(Shakes essays at him).*

PETER. *(pretending to peer closely).* If those include the essay I glanced at last night, on *Lady Windermere's Fan.* By some Swiss or Swede or Frog. Or Hun or Finn or other Wog. He concludes that Oscar Wilde was a bit of a humbugger. You know darling, they really shouldn't have to pay you for reading, you really ought to pay them for writing, lines like that. *(Reaches behind, pours scotch into his glass).*

HILARY. Is it any good telling you you'll be sorry in the morning, if you drink that.

PETER. I'll be sorry now, if I don't.

HILARY. Not too nice though, for Jeremy, at breakfast.

PETER. Then I shan't let him have it for breakfast.

HILARY. *(makes to go to door, stops, comes back)* Just because *you've* started being contemptuous of your work, don't you dare start showing me your contempt for mine. Because not only am I not contemptuous of it, no I'm not, but also—

PETER. Perhaps you should practise a *little* contempt for it. Taking it seriously is beginning to affect your conversational style. That last sentence was like the other half of a simultaneous translation.

HILARY. I started to tell you something and I'm going to finish.

PETER. OK. But keep your head. Now—'not only do you have a job which not only are you not contemptuous of, no you're not, but also—' Can you pick it up from there? But also?

HILARY. But also I have this home to run, and I'm sick to death of your contempt for that too. It's a difficult enough proposition at the best of times, but it's virtually impossible since you've taken to sneering at me for trying to do it while refusing to make even a gesture towards actually helping.

PETER. Actually helping in what?

HILARY. Everything. As for instance taking Jeremy to school *and* fetching him. Every day. With four hours hard teaching in between. Then there's the ironing, some of which you actually used to do at one time, remember, the *twice-* a-week drag through Sainsbury's now that you refuse to accompany me for one *big* load on Saturdays, then the cooking for Jeremy at tea-time, and preparing something for you later on, with tomorrow's teaching to get ready in the evening. On top of which I still do my best to look attractive—

PETER. On top of which on top of what, out of that assortment of recriminations and accolades? I know what else you've been doing, you sly-boots you, you've been mugging up on the rhetoric of the new woman. A tirade in the form of a *curriculum vitae*. Wherever have you found the time? *(Pause)* Actually, now you mention them, some of those meals you've been preparing recently were first prepared by Indians or Chinese, in those take-away restaurants. All you've had to do was to bring them home and then take them away. Usually uneaten. Before throwing them out. Why, if Charlie's doggie knew about your catering arrangements, he'd give up Headmaster's garden and lope straight up Muswell Hill.

HILARY. *(after a long pause)* Tell me—how long *do* you intend to keep this up?

PETER. What up?

HILARY. This—this pose of yours.

PETER. What pose of mine?

HILARY. I don't know what you're aiming at, but the result is somewhere between Falstaff and a spiteful woman columnist.

PETER. Falstaff? But I was only aiming for the spiteful woman columnist. *(Shakes his head effeminately)*

HILARY. God, I wish you knew how you looked.

PETER. A wish you're about to make come true, from the look of you. *(Settles back as if comfortably).* Well?

HILARY. You've got a—what?—two-day stubble over your face, your eyes are blood-shot, you've got a smoker's cough, which I've been hearing develop almost by the week. *(Pause).* Like your paunch.

PETER. You've been hearing my paunch develop? So that's why you've been sleeping so far down the bed, eavesdropping?

HILARY. No, keeping away from your breath. Which reeks of nicotine and booze.

PETER. Now that's dandruff, bad breath, smoker's cough, stubble and paunch. *(Ticking them off on his fingers).* But those details apart, do you find me as winsome as ever?

HILARY. I find you quite disgusting.

PETER. Careful sweetling, or in a second you'll say something you'll regret.

HILARY. I regret not having said it to you weeks ago. I don't know what's the matter with you, but I can't stand it any more. Not the sight of you, nor the nagging it provoked from me at first, nor the contempt I've felt for you recently. Because *that's* what my contempt has been for, *you.* We haven't been to a dinner party recently at which you haven't ended up drunker than anyone else, or any social occasion at which you haven't contrived to insult half the people in the room. I've been ashamed.

PETER. Well, some of those rooms were pretty large. Look at it this way, if they'd been half the size I'd have managed to insult the lot.

HILARY. But you haven't done it with style, Peter, don't delude yourself.

PETER. Quantity these days darling, a lot of those people I scarcely knew.

HILARY. But why? Why? *(Pause).* Today, with *your* brother and his family around—I don't know what you said to him when he came in here, but he was in a dreadful state when he came out—and before that at lunch, the way you sat lolling forward, your eyes glassy with too much drink and too much food—

PETER. And too much boredom! Don't forget the too much boredom!

HILARY. The real bore was you! Stirring yourself only to bait Charlie, completely ignoring Alison—

PETER. Not fair! I tried to bait Alison too. She chose to ignore it.

HILARY. I can't go on like this!

PETER. Really? I thought you were just warming up.

HILARY. You're poisoning my life. And Jeremy's. He doesn't even want you to read to him in the evenings any more. He actually cried when I said tonight you might be doing it. Or does that make you pleased with yourself too? *(Pause).* Neither of us can bear you as you are.

PETER. Well, neither of you will get me as I might have been, because that's over. And as for how I *was*—

HILARY. *(after a pause).* Well?

PETER. That's over too, so far over I've forgotten how I did it.

HILARY. Very well. *(Turns, goes towards the door).*

PETER. Oh, just a minute darling! *(Gets up, goes towards her, stands staring at her, then begins to unbutton her blouse).*

HILARY. What are you doing?

PETER. Stripping you down. *(Stops, then puts his arms around HILARY, pulls her to him, kisses her).* Before having you off.

HILARY beats him off savagely.

Hey—hey—*(Defending himself)* this is fun! *(Advances on her again).*

HILARY. *(strikes out at him again).* Stop it, stop it, stop it!

PETER backs away. They stand, breathing heavily, staring at each other.

How dare you!

PETER. How dare I what?

HILARY. Grab at me as if I were—I were—*(Slight pause, then witheringly)* like some dirty old man.

PETER. But you're not at all like some dirty old man. If you were I'd grab him instead. *(Little pause).* Well, it *is* Sunday, isn't it? And therefore about the hour for our Sunday evening sex. Distinguishable from our Wednesday evening sex by its venue. Wednesday evening's workaday sex, upstairs in bed after a dinner out. *If* we can arrange a baby-sitter *and* you have no marking to do. Sunday evening's Sabbatical sex down here on the sofa in a spontaneous tussle *after* you've shyly slipped off the sofa cover. *(Little pause).* At least so it used to be not too long ago.

HILARY. Well, not any more.

PETER. Now let's see—that's no cooking any more and no love-making any more—

HILARY. Love-making? You haven't made love to me for months. You just use me as a stage towards one of your post-coital cigarettes. That is, when you've been conscious. Otherwise you merely roll on top of me yawning and away from me snoring—

36

PETER. What do you do between my yawn and my snore, I wonder, in the short period when I tend to be quite active? Draw up your Sainsbury's shopping list or practise one of those pronunciation classes you give to Spanish nuns and other lay-abouts? I recall catching the odd murmur, though your limbs remain supine.

HILARY. It wasn't a murmur. It was a mutter.

PETER. But what? Directions? Encouragement?

HILARY. Hurry up pig, or get it over with. That sort of encouragement.

PETER. I see. Less of an effort then than actually resisting.

HILARY. At least quicker than all the rows and explanations that dragged on until dawn.

PETER. Which you now, you ageing paradox you, seem bent on having. Well then, let's discuss your past bedtime *froideurs*—the ones that led to the rows, and for which everything from Victorian headaches to brutally contemporary ailments were offered in explanation.

HILARY. The most usual explanation was that I was tired after a day out at work and a day of domestic duties. A simple matter which you were incapable of understanding—

PETER. Which, I suppose, is why you had to put more effort into a normal marital fuck.

HILARY. Do you honestly mean that you're going in for all this—smoking and drinking and spite—to make up for your sex-life?

PETER. My lack of it, perhaps.

HILARY. How childish you really are.

PETER. Well—well—do you think it's been fun sharing a bed with you.

HILARY. Then don't. *(Pause)*. Will you stay down here, please.

PETER. Certainly not! *You* stay down here, I'm off to the conjugating bed, as one of your Frogs or wogs would doubtless put it.

HILARY. If you prefer. I just didn't think it would be fair to separate you from your bottle.

PETER. Or yourself from Jeremy. Having two males beside you in bed has given you delusions of old-fashioned womanhood. But what lures him to slide between us most nights is only a nightmare after all. As he'll find out post-puberty.

HILARY. Which is it to be? Down here or upstairs.

PETER. I'll take down here. In my suddenly converted Muswell Hill maisonette bed-sitter, thank you.

HILARY. Right. *(Turns, goes out of the door, left)*.

PETER. *(following her, shouts up after her)*. So. You're replacing mechanical sex with spontaneous frigidity. *(Waits. There is a slight pause, then)*

Sounds of JEREMY crying.

PETER stands listening with growing uncertainty.

HILARY. *(re-appears)*. You've woken him. Does that complete your day's work? *(Goes out again)*.

PETER surges across the room as if to shut the door with a slam. Holds his hand, listens.

HILARY. *(off)*. It's all right, darling, nothing to be frightened of. Mummy's coming.

PETER. Sounds bloody frightening to me. *(Closes the door, goes to the drinks table, pours himself a large scotch, squirts soda water into it, drains it off. At the top of his voice).* I consider myself free at last! Absolutely free! *(Hurls the glass against a wall).*

Lights.

Scene Two

A small and depressing bed-sitter in, say, Chalk Farm. Bathroom off.

A cupboard-type kitchen on, concealed by a curtain. A chair by the bed, a desk, a tatty armchair. Books and magazines scattered about, and on the wall some Marxist-type posters. Ancient copies of the Daily Worker *and more recent ones of the* Worker's Press.

It is about eleven in the morning. PETER, *dressed except for his shirt, emerges from the bathroom, in which he has evidently been shaving. He is carrying a tin mug of Nescafé, from which he sips. He sits down on the bed to put on his shoes.*

There is a knock at the door.

PETER. Christ! *(Looks at his watch).* Just coming! *(He pulls on his shirt, buttons it up, knots his tie, runs his hands through his hair, races over to the bed, pulls up the covers, makes a futile attempt to clean up the mess).* On my way! *(Gives up, goes towards the door,* *stops, looks at his shoulders, brushes dandruff off them).* You're nice and early. *(Opening the door).* Oh.

CHARLES. Can I come in?

PETER steps aside with reluctance, lets CHARLES in.

I didn't really expect to catch you in. I thought you'd be at work.

PETER. I didn't really expect you to catch me in. I thought you'd be at work.

CHARLES. Actually, I've got a free morning. At least until lunch, when I have to see Headmaster.

PETER. Have to, do you, Charlie?

CHARLES. *Want* to, actually, Pete. It's a personal matter.

PETER. Really? What?

CHARLES. *(after a little pause).* I don't mind at all telling you. Bursar says there's a house opposite the school, quite a large one. And as Alison and I realise we need a larger place, I thought I'd ask Headmaster about the chances of getting it.

PETER. Rent free, would it be?

CHARLES. A nominal rent.

PETER. Well, I can see that if you don't believe in contraceptives, you've got to go in for family planning.

CHARLES. Perhaps I simply take my responsibilities seriously. To my family as well as my work. Or are you giving that up, too?

PETER. Isn't there some Froggy epigram to the effect that we don't give up our vices—they give us up?

CHARLES. *(shocked).* Do you mean you've been sacked?

PETER. Why should I be sacked, I haven't done anything. For weeks. Oh don't worry Charlie, we're having our six simultaneous publications party today. By two o'clock they won't remember that they didn't see me at ten o'clock, by three o'clock they won't even remember that they did see me at two. Drink?

CHARLES. At this hour?

PETER. Ah, but I've got some — *(Taking a syphon of soda from behind the curtain, holding it out temptingly. Then a bottle of scotch for himself. As he does so)* Like it, my bachelor pad?

CHARLES. Isn't it a bit out of date for a bachelor?

PETER. Yes, but then so am I. It belongs to one of our middle-aged Northern working-class authors. *(Squirting soda for CHARLES, pouring scotch and squirting soda for himself)*. I had him commissioned back to Wigan Pier, wherever that is, for a few months. To flatten down his prose and fire up his politics after his long stint as beer correspondent, or something, for the *Worker's Press* or whatever. *(Hands CHARLES his glass)*. I suppose Hilary sent you?

CHARLES. No. She didn't want me to come.

PETER. Although telling you where I was to be found, eh?

CHARLES. No, she refused. I happened to stumble on that extraordinary post card you sent her.

PETER. It was a perfectly ordinary change of address card.

CHARLES. With an obscene drawing on it.

PETER. Well it was done from memory. And where did you happen to stumble on it, Charlie? In her handbag?

CHARLES. No, in the waste-paper basket. Hilary has no idea I'm here. *(Little pause)*. Is it any use asking you to explain.

PETER. Explain what?

CHARLES. Why you've left Hilary.

PETER. Certainly, as it's easily explained. She asked me to leave her bed and I kept on going—right out of the house. All right?

CHARLES. No, it's damned well not all right—for one thing, what about Jeremy?

PETER. Oh, she won't be turning *him* out of her bed for some years yet, if then.

CHARLES: Look Pete, I've been thinking—is it because of her job? You don't resent that, do you? Because you feel less important now that she's meeting new people— her colleagues—?

PETER. Oh, they don't sound particularly new. In fact, most of them sound old and weary, except for the students, who just sound foreign.

CHARLES. Oh come on Pete, come on, I don't believe it's as simple as it seems. You didn't just start going to seed and then turning nasty, and then walked out or were asked to leave—not just like that. There must be something really terrible between you suddenly, after so many years of happy marriage. What is it?

PETER. Oh, perhaps just so many years of happy marriage between us, eh Charlie? And perhaps so many turned out to be more than our fair share.

CHARLES. And that's all you'll say?

PETER. What does Hilary say?

CHARLES. Nothing. Except that it's for the best.

PETER. *(after a pause).* Well there you are. In accord to the very end.

CHARLES. And so what now? What do you do now? *(Angrily).* This—this bachelor pad and a return to your old ways.

PETER. What old ways?

CHARLES. Your promiscuous old ways. Do you really think at your age you can just go back to a life of short affairs and what was that hideous phrase you used to use—easy lays. Well, you're not an Oxford undergraduate any longer Peter, you won't find it easy with the Gertas—.

PETER. Gerta? Who's Gerta?

CHARLES. Frieda, whoever she was, that German ballerina.

PETER. Oh, Gretel it was. Wasn't it?

CHARLES. *(contemptuously).* And that Italian painter who was old enough to be your mother. Do you think it's going to be like that all over again. And that wretched business with André Gide's daughter.

PETER. André Gide's daughter! *(Laughs).* Charlie, I assure you, André Gide never had a daughter.

CHARLES. Well some French writer who was in vogue a dozen years ago. Well you're a married man now, that's what you are.

PETER. Am I? Charlie, you know nothing about any of it.

CHARLES. Don't I? I remember the states you used to get into. It's a lucky thing for you you married Hilary when you did—your bachelor days nearly killed you.

PETER. Now I've got them back, perhaps they'll finish

the job. You're not still jealous, are you Charlie, of those old passions of mine?

CHARLES. Jealous? What should *I* be jealous of?

PETER. Well you never slept with a woman before you married Alison, did you? You had no premarital sex at all, did you? Well, did you?

CHARLES. As a matter of fact I did, yes.

PETER. You didn't! Christ, who with?

CHARLES. Alison.

PETER. Why, you *rascal!* You used to boast that yours was a *real* wedding night, in the old-fashioned sense of the term. Which I always took to mean a disaster, by the way.

CHARLES. It only happened the once. One Sunday in my room in Reading we went—without meaning to— we went all the way. Afterwards we talked the whole thing through and decided that what with Alison's Catholicism and Mummy's desperation about your behaviour *and* my own—no doubt from your point of view, simple-minded—principles, I'd have to control myself a little.

PETER. A *little?* That's not very flattering to either of you. Anyway, Charlie, you see how unqualified you are to judge other people's sexual lives. Your own having consisted of ten years of marriage to Alison, preceded by two or three years of light to heavy necking with Alison (apart from that interrupting coitus) preceded by *(Little pause)* Jane Russell, wasn't it? Into a jam jar.

There is a pause.

CHARLES. How did you know that?

PETER. What?

CHARLES. About the—the—.

PETER. Jane Russell jam-jar? Mummy told me you'd confessed.

CHARLES. When?

PETER. After she'd interrogated you about the jam-jar and the Jane Russells she found under your floorboards.

CHARLES. But when did she tell you?

PETER. Oh, immediately after I'd confessed. Which was after she'd interrogated me about the old sock and the Betty Grables she found on top of my cupboard. But why look so troubled, Charlie, everybody wanked at Wundale, including most of the staff, from a memory of their complexions. That scandal when it was discovered that some of the older boarders had established it as a competitive sport and were awarding House Colours?

CHARLES. It's not that. It's just that she promised me she'd never say a word about it to anyone, especially you.

PETER. And I promised her I'd never tell you she told me. So now we're all square, two decades on. What exactly did she say to you?

CHARLES. That if I went on doing it, I'd never get into the Wundale First for soccer.

PETER. And she was quite right, you didn't. Although I suppose you didn't go on masturbating, either?

CHARLES. What did she say to you?

PETER. That I'd ruin my eyes, lose my concentration, and wouldn't get a scholarship to Oxford. Of course, I didn't know then what Oxford was like, or I'd have settled for spectacles and a few O-levels.

CHARLES. You were bloody lucky to get into Oxford.

PETER. Really? Your line used to be that Reading was just as good.

CHARLES. Indeed it was. And is. You were lucky to get into Oxford because you'd never have got through the interview at Reading. You were far too pretentious for us at eighteen—especially the way you worked at it.

PETER. I know. That's why I worked at it.

CHARLES. *(after a pause).* Anyway, how dare you confuse my attitudes to sex with Mummy's. Do you seriously believe I'd make that sort of mistake with *my* children? You wouldn't find a more enlightened attitude to masturbation than Headmaster's and mine at Amplesides.

PETER. Except possibly at the cinemas and theatres.

CHARLES. I'm not against sex, I'm very much for it— *good* sex, that is. Which is what one has, lovingly, with those one loves.

PETER. Such as oneself?

CHARLES. Oh ha ha. Anyway, this is all a waste of time—as I take it you haven't left Hilary because she won't allow you to masturbate. Not that I don't know what you're up to, oh I knew straight away really, and so did Alison. She said the only question was whether you'd started sleeping around again, or whether there was a particular girl. Although, as she also said, the girl wouldn't be too particular to want you as you are now. *(Pause).* Well, which is it? *(Pause).* For how long and with how many have you been committing adultery?

46

PETER. Committing—*(Laughs) committing* adultery. Oh Charlie *(Shakes his head)*. One isn't *allowed* to commit it these days, it's stopped qualifying as a sin. Why, for lots of blokes in publishing it's become such a habit that half of them don't even enjoy it. For instance, it's an open secret that one of our Senior Editors always takes his lady authors to bed instead of to lunch, so that he can spend the expenses another day on his grown-up daughter by his first marriage. Three marriages back. That's all that's meant by a permissive society now, Charlie, an arrangement with a restaurant. I believe he has some deal with his male authors too, but that secret's closed. Good God, brother, all our friends, Hilary's and mine—and *her* colleagues too, at that language school, I'll bet—they're all having affairs or have had them and are moving on to separations and divorces, which, by the way, sound far less hum-drum than the adulteries that led up to them. There's only one marriage I can think of that's survived as long as yours and mine — and that's Jeff and Davina Wainright's.

CHARLES. The Wainwrights! You mean those ghastly people you had us to dinner with—he was drunk, as I remember, and she was crying in the lavatory, Alison discovered, over some long-drawn-out affair he was having, you told us so yourself, afterwards. Is that your idea of a good marriage?

PETER. No, only of a settled one. If his mistresses left him, his wife would go too. She couldn't stand the conversational vacuum—or having him home so early in the evenings.

47

CHARLES. I remember distinctly your telling me you'd stopped liking the Wainwrights.

PETER. But that was years ago.

CHARLES. And now you like them again?

PETER. God no. I've merely realised that they're among our oldest friends, and that old friends are like old habits. It doesn't matter whether you like them, they're what you've got. Until somebody introduces a really useful trade paper at least—new friends wanted, old ones offered in part exchange.

CHARLES. What have the Wainwrights got to do with all this anyway?

PETER. Absolutely nothing, as they're still together. But the rest of our friends, Charlie, over the eight years during which Hilary and I have idled and dallied together, have been busy splitting up and re-grouping. Why, in at least three cases we've actually been lapped. Double divorces are becoming as fashionable as separate holidays.

CHARLES. *(with total contempt)*. So you've left Hilary to be fashionable, have you?

PETER. Possibly. Or possibly to be free of something that neither of us could stand any longer.

CHARLES. *(gestures around the room)*. Free! You call *this* free.

PETER. Yup. Not even a nominal rent, Charlie.

CHARLES. You know why you're a bloody fool, Peter? Not for moral reasons, or conventional or *unconventional* ones, as they are nowadays, to do with the sanctity of family life and the squalors of easy sex—not those. But simply that you're on your way to losing your wife and your son both of whom you love. You can't go back to your pre-married life, and you can't behave like all these others you cite—and I'll tell you why. At bottom your nature is as affectionate as mine. So one day, probably very soon, you'll go back to Hilary, and it'll be too late. The damage will have been done. *(Pause)*. It's true, isn't it? You *do* love Hilary?

There is a knock at the door.

PETER. Ah, excuse me, Charlie, can we leave that question hanging while I open the door. *(Opens it)*.

JOANNA. Hello. Sorry I'm late.

PETER. Oh don't worry—I was in no danger of giving you up. This is my brother Charlie.

JOANNA. Hello.

PETER. Joanna's one of our free-lance cover designers. I've asked her to accompany me to the party.

JOANNA. It'll be the first real publishing do I've ever wormed my way into.

PETER. Then we mustn't miss a minute of it. Shall we go?

CHARLES. Just a minute—*(Takes a photograph out of his pocket, hands it to PETER)*. Something I was going to leave for you if you weren't in.

PETER. Ah, a *memento mori*. Well, as I *was* in, you can take it away again.

CHARLES. It belongs to you.

PETER. Did you retrieve it from the waste-paper basket too?

CHARLES. No, it was on our piano. Alison took it last summer.

PETER. I don't want it, Charlie.

CHARLES. Why not? Does it upset you?

JOANNA. God, what's it of, anyway?

CHARLES. It's a photograph of my brother's wife and child. *(Hands it to JOANNA).*

JOANNA. *(studies it).* Taken with an instamatic, right?

PETER. *(takes the photograph back, hands it to CHARLES).* It belongs to Alison, I believe we've established. Can't she find room for it in her waste-paper basket. *(Holds the door open for JOANNA).*

JOANNA and CHARLES stare at each other. CHARLES coldly, JOANNA puzzled. She goes out.

PETER keeps holding the door open for CHARLES, who doesn't move. Then he goes out.

CHARLES. *(stands trembling for a second, then goes to the soda syphon, squirts himself some).* The little— the little—*(Gulps down the soda water, pulls himself together, then goes over, places the photograph on the table, by the bed. Exits).*

Lights half down.

Lights up.

PETER enters, followed by JOANNA, They are both slightly drunk, and laughing.

JOANNA. Christ, no truly, you were devastating. I've never heard anyone put so many people down before. But then I've never seen so many intellectuals before— are all publishing parties like that?

PETER. *(who is getting out the scotch).* It was a special occasion. We were launching a coffee table book on Sir Alf Ramsey Must Go. One of six simultaneous cultural publications. If you buy the lot we throw the coffee table in free, along with a ghosted autobiography of the late Lord Chamberlain and a portfolio of photographs of Henry Cooper's greatest defeats.

JOANNA. Henry Cooper the boxer? Was he the bloke that made the speech?

PETER. No, that was the new Chairwoman of the Arts Council.

JOANNA. It wasn't!

PETER. No it wasn't. I'm just fantasising to distract our attention.

JOANNA. What from?

PETER. The party. Drink? *(Pours himself one, squirts in soda water).*

JOANNA lets out a peal of laughter.

Something?

JOANNA. No, just remembering the way you put down that specimen who was praising up somebody's books—

PETER. Nuzek's?

JOANNA. Nuzek's, right. 'Why Cyril, I didn't know you had a lisp', you said.

PETER. *(laughs, stops).* But he hasn't got a lisp, old Cyril. Has he?

JOANNA. No, he hasn't, that was why you said it. Because *he* said if Nuzek's latest was like his last it was bound to be full of pith. Then you said, why Cyril—

51

PETER. Got it. Got it, got it.

JOANNA. It took *me* two minutes to get it at the time.

PETER. Then Cyril was a mite quicker than you, if memory serves. Which it suddenly insists on doing, now you've set it in motion. Like some uncontrollably obsequious waiter . . . *(Sits down)*.

JOANNA. He didn't know which way to turn when you'd finished with him, who was he?

PETER. One of the Sunday reviewers. Unlike his colleagues, he'll know which way to turn come Nuzek's Sunday, a year hence.

JOANNA. And that lady—she marched out when you were telling everybody that story about some creep who takes writers to bed instead of lunch—I thought it was brilliant, who was she anyway?

PETER. What did she look like exactly?

JOANNA. Tall and grey haired with a hat and a see-through.

PETER. Our Senior Editor's third wife.

JOANNA. And that little creep with the goatee and the beady eyes—

PETER. That was the Senior Editor. His eyes aren't usually beady. They're usually twinkly.

JOANNA. Well, they were beady from the moment we arrived and you told that joke about Nu Nude—what was it again?

PETER. Nuzek. Nu-zek.

JOANNA. His bottom copy going on a five-year-old bottom, so the paper hadn't been wasted after all. It nearly brought the house down.

PETER. It still might.

JOANNA. Most people really enjoyed you, except those and that little roly-poly bloke—the one with the foreign accent standing next to me for a bit—he really hated you. Who was he?

PETER. A roly Pole called Nuzek. Nu-zek. Oh Christ.

JOANNA. What's the matter?

PETER. Nothing. Absolutely nothing.

JOANNA. And the Horatio Bottomley of Women's Lib—I never thought I'd see *her* cry, I mean I'm on her side really, and that man that was with her—

PETER. Look, look, I don't really need a list, thanks very much. The names are winging in, in flocks and unaided.

JOANNA. Hey, you're not sorry or anything, are you?

PETER. Sorry! *(Laughs).* No, no, it's only that it's a long time since I struck out without making sure of hitting only air or a loved one. *(Goes over to her).* Besides, haven't we better things to do *(Lurches slightly)* than reminisce over my past before it's properly begun. *(Puts his arms around her, kisses her. Whispers in her ear. Pause, looks at her apprehensively).* Eh, what do you say?

JOANNA. All right. Great. *(Goes over to the bed, sits down, begins to undress).*

PETER looks towards her, then also begins to get undressed.

(Who has been staring at the picture as she undresses). How old's your wife anyway?

PETER. What? *(Sees the picture).* Oh. Um, thirty-one and a half.

JOANNA. Your boy's what, five?

PETER. Nearly six. That was taken a year ago.

JOANNA. *(picks up the picture).* What's she look like? It's hard to tell because she's out of focus.

PETER. *(going over in trousers and shirt).* Can we keep her that way, do you mind? *(Taking the picture from JOANNA).* To avoid pre- and even coital depression. *(Comes back with the picture, drops it on the floor).* I'm free now, you know.

They go on undressing, on opposite sides of the room.

Lights.

CURTAIN

Act Two

Scene One

The bed-sitter. Some time later. JOANNA is sitting on the bed in her under-pants, doing up her bra. PETER is on the chair, in vest and trousers, pulling on his socks. He stops, sits staring blankly ahead, then fumbles in his jacket pocket (which is slung over the back of the chair) for his cigarettes. Takes one out.

JOANNA. *(who has been watching him).* I've got some pot, if you want. *(Taking a small box out of her hand-bag, beside the bed).*

PETER. What? *(Sitting down, not looking at her).*

JOANNA. Do you want a joint?

PETER. No thanks. I find these much more exciting. *(Lights up, drags deeply, coughs).* Don't need the police to be frightened of them.

JOANNA. *(putting a joint between her lips).* Can I have a light then?

PETER. What? Oh sorry. *(Half turns, tosses her the lighter without looking at her. It falls to one side).* Sorry.

JOANNA lights up, also drags deeply into her lungs.

They sit smoking for a short while. PETER coughs once or twice.

JOANNA. You've had a bad scene going recently, haven't you?

PETER grunts.

Look, if it helps, I'm just getting over one, too. *(Pause).* But it's just a matter of time, that's all. I've got to the stage, you know, where I can tell myself it's over without even weeping. Dead. Terminado. Finito. Finished. Not that anything ever finishes, right? Christ, we were even going to get married!

PETER. That would have finished it.

JOANNA. His name was Josh.

PETER. Look, you really don't have to talk about it if you don't want to.

JOANNA. No, I want to.

PETER. Then I suppose it's irrelevant that you don't have to.

JOANNA. Right. *(After a pause).* Witby.

PETER. Whatby?

JOANNA. Josh Witby . . . He directed the all black, all male *Way of the World* for the *Cellar in the Underground*, Islington. You know, the place where they guarantee your 30p. back if you don't like it and they have those posters up saying find out about experimental drama, it's only two hours of your life.

PETER. Can they guarantee those back?

JOANNA. *(laughs. There is a pause).* My rival was Lady What's it, Wishfort, get it?

PETER. Got it. Witby's Lady Wishfort is all black and part male.

JOANNA. Josh's problem in a nutshell.

PETER. Sounds an excellent place for it.

JOANNA. I like sleeping with men, and so does he.

PETER. You have that much in common, at least. Most marriages start from far less.

JOANNA. Listen, I haven't got anything against homosexuals.

PETER. Nor have I. Even as bed-partners for heterosexuals.

JOANNA. And nothing against black boys either.

PETER. Nor have I. Even in parts written for white women in restoration comedies.

JOANNA. Well, you sound as if you've got something against someone, is it me?

PETER. No, nothing against you either, and you're white, female and we've just shared a bed together. How tolerant do I have to be?

JOANNA. Bet you can't even bring yourself to look at me, can you?

PETER. Sorry. *(Turns, looks at her, looks away again).* I am sorry. It must be that pre-coital depression I was worried about. It's struck.

JOANNA. But truly it doesn't matter. I don't mind.

PETER. Good. Unfortunately I do.

JOANNA. *(comes over to him).* But you don't have to sit around like a sick dog, I mean the way you got out of bed and into your knickers—it was almost as bad as the way you got out of them—all doubled up and walking across the room in a crouch. You were ashamed before we even started, what of?

PETER. I think it must have been my paunch.

JOANNA. You know what you did while you were—I mean, you actually proposed to me.

PETER. Oh, you heard that, did you. I tried to make it sound like a love-cry. *(Pause)*. If you'd accepted on a *pro-tem* basis, things might have ended differently.

JOANNA. Perhaps, if you hadn't drunk so much, you might have done it.

PETER. Perhaps if I hadn't drunk so much, I wouldn't have tried.

JOANNA. Thank you. Thank you. *(Grinds out her cigarette)*. Oh Christ, this is all a lot of balls.

PETER. You don't need a lot, actually one will do. Bull-fighters manage on even less, so they say.

JOANNA. This hasn't happened to you before then, never?

PETER. No.

JOANNA. Never with your wife, even?

PETER. Not even. Except in Paris on our honeymoon, when I pretended for a fatal fraction of a thrust that we were on a dirty weekend.

JOANNA. Look, am I the only girl since you were married, apart from your wife?

PETER says nothing.

Well, am I? *(Little pause)*. I am, aren't I? Right?

PETER. Right, right. You're the only girl I've had apart from my wife. Right?

JOANNA. Wrong. You didn't have me. Right?

PETER. Right. Thank you. I'd forgotten your gift for instant recall. Perhaps because I try so hard to lack it myself.

JOANNA. What were you doing, practising! Christ! *(Goes to the rest of her clothes, begins to put them on).* You know what you are, you're the type—.

PETER. Don't bother. I *know* the type. *(Gets up, puts on shirt, etc.).* I gather all the other married men you've slept with have managed to come good.

JOANNA. But then they enjoyed it, too.

PETER. Even the guilt?

JOANNA. Even the sex. There was one I knew, he'd phone his wife from my bed and pretend he was at his desk. He even pretended to be the porter on the switch-board sometimes. *(Suddenly laughs).* He used to say the best planned lays never gang agly.

PETER. And what happened to that little idyll?

JOANNA. His wife found out.

PETER. And put a stop to it pretty sharpish, right?

JOANNA. Wrong. As soon as he knew she knew he lost interest.

PETER. So he didn't want you, he just wanted the situation?

JOANNA. That was kind of you, to explain. What makes you think *I* wanted *you,* and not just the situation?

PETER. So that's why you limit yourself to a Josh on the one hand, or to married men on the other? But there's a large variety of males between homos and husbands, you know. When are you going to have a go at one of those?

JOANNA. I don't limit myself at all—except when I end up in the sack with somebody like you. Christ, there was a time today when I truly liked you—at the party, I thought you had something then, but it was just words, wasn't it, and then you had to be drunk to do it. I just hope you haven't given *me* anything catching, that's all.

PETER. What? Oh, you mean my inhibitions? But they don't get passed on by casual contact, only through an intimacy that digs deep into tissues you seem to have been born without. No, don't you worry, dear, you'll still be able to sleep around, smoke pot, promote your new jargons, bury our old language, and generally see our dying culture underground, right down to Josh's cellar—where my son—my son—*(Stands shaking)*.

JOANNA. *(looks at him. Laughs).* And I was only talking about your dandruff. *(Goes out).*

PETER. *(after a moment).* So was I. *(Looks at shoulders, left and right, brushes futilely at them).*

Lights Down

Lights Up

Scene Two

Muswell Hill. It is evening, about eight o'clock. Lights on.

HILARY enters left.

JEREMY off, left, calls out something.

HILARY. *(at the door).* No more cuddles tonight, you don't mean it anyway, sleep now. And no sneaking into my bed.

Listens, sounds of JEREMY off, complaining. HILARY smiles, goes across to the desk, picks up her brief case, sits down at the desk, opens it. Takes out some papers, begins to look through them. Stops. Sits staring ahead.

There is a sudden rap on the window.

HILARY lets out a little scream. There is a crashing at the kitchen, and as HILARY rises in alarm, CHARLES enters.

CHARLES. Hello, I thought I'd come this way so as not to disturb.

HILARY. Thank you.

CHARLES. In case Jeremy was asleep.

HILARY. Yes.

CHARLES. Actually it's the pot. Nindy's pot. We left it here that Sunday—and Nindy's suddenly taken against the old one, after using it for the last week. I don't know why, but she wants *hers* back. Alison's had to use the old sink ploy with the tap running—anyway I thought I'd just pop over and get it. You know? *(Little pause).* I should have phoned.

HILARY. It's very nice to see you. I'll go and get it. *(Goes off, left).*

CHARLES goes to the drinks table.

Makes to squirt some soda water into a glass. The syphon farts emptily. CHARLES studies the bottom of the syphon, then raises the syphon, bending slightly at the knees, puts the tube into his mouth, and squirts and sucks.

HILARY re-entering with the pot, watches him from the the door.

CHARLES not seeing, puts the syphon down.

HILARY. Here you are. *(Hands him the pot).*

CHARLES. Thanks.

HILARY. *(after a pause).* Would you like a drink?

CHARLES. No, no thanks. Well, just some soda water, if there is any.

HILARY. I think it's empty.

CHARLES. There isn't another one in the cupboard— Pete—sometimes there's a spare in the cupboard.

HILARY. *(goes to the cupboard, looks).* No.

CHARLES. Oh.

HILARY. Something else perhaps? There's some lime, or squash or ribena . . . ?

CHARLES. No, no thanks. I like soda water, you see. Its taste.

HILARY. But surely it doesn't have any taste.

CHARLES. Yes, that's what I like. And the way the bubbles shoot up against the roof of the mouth—

HILARY. Well, some coffee—or something to eat?

CHARLES. No, I had a nut and spinach cutlet before coming out. With boiled potatoes and blackberries. The blackberries were for pudding.

HILARY. Charlie—are we having this awkward conversation because you can't get into another awkward conversation you feel we should have. It occurred to me to check the waste-paper basket after you left. Have you come to report on your meeting?

CHARLES. He wasn't in, so I have nothing to report. *(Pause).* Is everything all right though, Hilary?

HILARY. As long as you don't start re-interrogating me. I still don't want to talk about it.

CHARLES. All right. *(Sits down).*

HILARY. It's very sweet of you to take it all so badly, but really I think it would be more helpful if you tried to take it well.

CHARLES. *(nods).* But I think he's a little—*(Checks himself).* Sorry Hilary. *(Sits in a sort of stupor).*

HILARY. Is there something else the matter? Alison's all right—?

CHARLES. Oh yes, yes. She's fine. *(Little pause).* Perhaps a touch of pre-natal depression.

HILARY. Oh dear. But that's unusual, isn't it? She's generally so exuberant just before.

CHARLES. No, I meant me. I always get a bit low—but I don't let Alison see, of course. Or anyone. But this time it's worse than usual—what with you and Pete—a double touch really. Appropriate as we're going to have twins.

HILARY. Twins! Why, Charlie, that's marvellous, twins! How wonderful.

CHARLES. I thought you knew.

HILARY. Yes, Alison did tell me, as a matter of fact. But she said she wasn't going to tell you, she wanted it to be a surprise.

CHARLES. Well, she couldn't resist after all. She told me this evening. I think to cheer me up over Pete and everything. *(Sits).*

HILARY. But Charlie, you don't mind, do you? Twins, just think—

CHARLIE. Oh, I'm sure once they're here. I wish she'd kept the surprise as a surprise though. Then I wouldn't have had time to prepare for it. Anyway I just used the pot as an excuse—I had to get away for a little, in case I couldn't cope. *(Little pause)*. It's monstrous of me to burden you with myself, isn't it?

HILARY. No, it isn't. I'm glad you came, it would be far more monstrous if Alison suspected—Charlie, you don't think a little whisky would help.

CHARLES. No, only a lot would. Sorry Hil. I suppose really it's an inevitable progression. We've been turning them out in singles for eight years, we were bound to advance. Recently in class I've taken to saying everything twice. Perhaps it was an early warning—

HILARY. Is it a matter of economics, your depression?

CHARLES. Well, I *have* got used to pacing them out in my mind and planning ahead. But if they're going to start coming in clusters—? What can I do?

HILARY. Couldn't you count this as two goes worth? Oh, of course, how silly of me, I'd forgotten Alison's Catholicism.

CHARLES. Her Catholicism's just a blind, Hilary. Lots of practising Catholics also practise contraception these days, while Alison scarcely bothers to practise Catholicism except in her attitude to contraceptives. When it comes down to it, the Pope's just her fertility symbol. She likes babies, lots and lots of babies. She likes cuddling them, burping them, changing them, feeding them, preferably while bearing them. *(Pause)*. Oh, I don't blame her, of course. I always knew she was a natural homemaker, it's one of the reasons I wanted to marry her. It's just that the house I'm paying the mortgage on isn't big enough for the home she's making. I haven't dared tell her yet—*(stops)*.

HILARY. What?

CHARLES. Well, there was a chance of a house that belongs to the school—much larger than ours and the rent would be nominal. Bursar was sure it could be arranged, but Headmaster said no.

HILARY. Why?

CHARLES. Oh, he was very nice about it, of course. He wants to start a new school house for boarders—perfectly sensible, really. But it's always a bit of a shock being turned down—*(Little pause)* especially—*(Lets out a little laugh)*.

HILARY. Charlie?

CHARLES. Can I tell you something, in great confidence?

HILARY. If you're sure I ought to know.

CHARLES. It's something ridiculous. Something very ridiculous. On the other hand it's not. You must try not to laugh, but I shan't blame you if you do. You see— I asked Headmaster about the house at lunch, but at tea I suddenly thought I'd look in on him, just for a cup and—well, I often do you know, to talk about co-education or scholarships—but this time I also wanted him to see that I perfectly understood about not getting the house. Well, we had a very affable chat together, his wife was there and we always get along very well—it was very pleasant, I thought, very pleasant.

HILARY. Well, it sounds very pleasant.

CHARLES. Yes, it was. And when I left I decided to walk back to the car through their garden. I often go that way, especially if it's a fine evening. I wasn't at all depressed then, you know, of course I didn't know about the twins—well, perhaps I was a little depressed about Pete, thinking what a fool he was and why he couldn't count his blessings—and then I began to count my own, you know, the way one does—miscounting, as it turned out. But I began to feel rather happy. Rather happy, that's my point.

HILARY. And why shouldn't you be. You've got a great deal to be happy about.

CHARLES. Exactly, I know. And I wished I had Pete there, because I was sure I could persuade him—when suddenly I heard Headmaster's voice. He was talking to his wife. They didn't see me—in fact, they must have thought I was long gone. I was just about to squeeze through some shrubs, to let them know where I was, I didn't want them to think I was eavesdropping—when I heard Headmaster say: 'But there must be some way of keeping the pest out of my house'.

HILARY. *(after a pause)*. Oh Charlie!

CHARLES. And his wife said: 'Oh, I know he's an appalling nuisance, but I can't help having a soft spot for him'.

HILARY. Oh Charles!

CHARLES. 'That's because he grovels whenever he sees you!' And then he said—

HILARY. Oh Charlie, don't go on. Please. I can't bear it.

CHARLES. Said 'The other day I saw him peeing over the roses. He's always squatting in the path and fouling it. He leaves fleas over the carpet, you've said so yourself.'

66

HILARY. They were talking about that stray—Alfonso! At least I hope they were.

CHARLES. So what it comes to is this. You don't think I have the physical habits of a dog, just the moral temperament of one.

HILARY. I think no such thing!

CHARLES. My God, I admired him though, for a moment.

HILARY. Headmaster?

CHARLES. Alfonso. I wished I could pee over his roses, drop turds on his path and shake fleas over his carpet. But I wouldn't grovel to his wife, I'd bite her ankles.

HILARY. I thought you liked them!

CHARLES. So did I. Until I thought I heard them talking about me like that.

HILARY. But they weren't talking about you. They were talking about Alfonso.

CHARLES. I know, I know. But you see, the fact that I *thought* they were talking about me must mean there's something in my idea of them that expects them to talk like that about me. And something in me that expects to be talked about like that. It's just the sort of thing I know Pete's always—*(Stops)*. Well anyway. But you know, almost the most shameful thing Hil—when I was in my car and well, trembling a little—a muddle of feelings, hate and anger for them, oh quite irrational, I realised it even at the time—but in the middle of all that I had this sudden very clear thought. Do you know what it was? Something *really* shameful?

HILARY. *(after a moment)*. I think so. That you'd better stop feeding Alfonso, now you know what Headmaster thinks of him.

CHARLES. *(nods, despairingly).* And a second later I imagined myself making some casual reference to the effect—that perhaps we ought to have something done about him.

HILARY. Put down, you mean? Oh Charlie!

CHARLES. If you met me now, for the first time, you wouldn't dream of asking me back to your house for dinner, would you?

HILARY. Of course I would.

CHARLES. No you wouldn't. Alison's very attached to you, you know.

HILARY. Yes, I do know.

CHARLES. Still, she thinks you're a conceited little turnip.

HILARY. Turnip?

CHARLES. Sometimes parsnip. She hates the way you prattle boastfully on about your job. That's the sort of thing she says about you, although she loves you. So what sort of things do you say about her, although you love her if you do. About her constant pregnancies, for example, or her earth-mother laugh—or her unattractiveness.

HILARY. I think she's *very* attractive!

CHARLES. What's so attractive about her?

HILARY. She's got a lovely, open face, a marvellous complexion.

CHARLES. And a dreadful figure.

HILARY. She has not!

CHARLES. Yes, she has. What isn't dreadful about it?

HILARY. For one thing, she's got absolutely beautiful breasts. So full.

CHARLES. Yes, well they usually are, aren't they? *(Little pause)*. What about her bottom?

HILARY. Charlie, this has gone on quite long enough.

CHARLES. Actually, her bottom isn't as baggy as it looks when she's wearing those pregnancy trousers she usually wears. *(Little pause)*. You don't think I hate her, do you?

HILARY. No. I know you love her.

CHARLES. But you hate hearing me say things like this about her?

HILARY. Yes. But I'd rather you said them to me than to her.

CHARLES. I'll stop in a minute. Honestly. But do you know what would make it all right for me, absolutely? If I could just go to bed some evenings, and stretch, and turn on the reading light, and sigh luxuriously, and open a book. An Arthur Ransome. I long to re-read all the Arthur Ransomes.

HILARY. Surely you can manage that?

CHARLES. Alison always goes up before me. Then when I come in she stretches, turns off the reading light, and gives a luxurious sigh, and opens her legs. *(Little pause)*. No, that's not true. We have a long cuddle first, which I need. But that's how it ends. Every night. We have this joke, that she can't get to sleep without it. And recently since we've gone macrobiotic there's been a joke about not being able to get up without it, either.

HILARY. But not *every* night, Charlie, it's not possible.

CHARLES. But then there are bottles to warm up, or nappies to be changed, or mid-night wee-wees, or six week cholic—Otherwise every night. You see, she loves everything to do with babies, but especially the way they're made.

HILARY. But couldn't you, well, just hint—?

CHARLES. Our marriage is constructed on our triumphant sex life, as you know. That, and our shared love of children.

HILARY. But you do *like* children. Don't you?

CHARLES. Nobody likes children these days. Why should I? They don't even like each other. But I love them, if that's what perpetually counting them and fretting for them and planning because of them amounts to. But I don't want to look at them, or hear them, let along watch them eat, empty their pots and nappies—

HILARY. You sound just like Peter.

CHARLES. Oh God, I wish I *were* just like him, or even better be him! *(Little pause).* Sorry Hilary, I wasn't referring to—to his current behaviour. But you see he's always been the younger one, the brighter one, the indulged one—the anarchic one. While I've just been the conventional one, the slow and loving and responsible one. The one-girl one. All those affairs he had before you—

HILARY. What? What affairs?

CHARLES. But surely he told you about them?

HILARY. No.

CHARLES. I shouldn't have spoken.

HILARY. No, I want to hear.

CHARLES. Are you sure?

HILARY. I want to hear.

CHARLES. But how could he have not confessed. The German ballerina, the Italian painter, Gide's daughter—

HILARY. *Gide's* daughter!

CHARLES. No, it wasn't Gide's, it was—I can't remember, a French writer. His daughter. The affaire of his life until he met you. And he never said a word?

HILARY. I'd forgotten. It was all so long ago.

CHARLES. I suppose it was. But it still makes me angry to think of them. Because, you see, secretly, I wanted them, and if I couldn't have them, I wanted him to. Just as—just as—well, although I've always loved Alison, but was never actually in love with her, so I've—I've always been in love with you. Though now I love you too as my sister-in-law. From the first moment he showed you off to me. But you know that, don't you?

HILARY nods.

But you belonged to Pete, of course. Just as I did to Alison. All four of us were perfectly matched. You had lots of affairs too, didn't you, before you married Pete?

HILARY. Lots?

CHARLES. Well, quite a few.

HILARY. I suppose quite a few, yes.

CHARLES. How many?

HILARY. *(after a pause).* Five, actually.

CHARLES. *(whistles).* Five! Alison's always said— *(Pause).* So you see, you *were* perfectly matched. Almost mathematically. While I was always the sort of chap to meet the sort of chap that Alison is, without having anything before—and that was that. *(Little pause)*. You've never been the slightest bit in love with me, have you?

HILARY shakes her head.

And perhaps that's why I can't help being a little glad that you and Pete have broken up. Oh, not only because of being in love with you, but also—this is my very last confession, Hil.

HILARY. Thank God!

CHARLES. Because it's easier for me to bear being what I am, a loving family man, an obsequious Assistant Headmaster in a minor Public School, a bit of an old-fashioned Puritan, if *he's* behaving despicably. I want him to live my destructive life for me, while I go on living my decent life for myself. Oh God, how shameful! I do want him to come back, I do, I do.

HILARY puts her face to one side. She is in tears.

Hil—Hil—Oh, I am sorry, I've been selfish. I'd no right —oh, don't cry, please. *(Comes over, puts an arm around her)*. Did I make you?

HILARY shakes her head.

CHARLES. Because of Pete and you?

HILARY. No, not especially, a little.

CHARLES. Because of Alison and me?

HILARY. A little, but not only.

CHARLES. Ah. *Lacrimae Rerum.* I felt them rising in me, when Alison was laughing over the twins, and I was trying to laugh with her. Pete will come back to you Hil. I know he loves you.

72

HILARY. So do I.

CHARLES. So you know he'll come back to you?

HILARY. Yes. I know it.

CHARLES. Then nothing's really too bad, is it?

Lights Down.

Lights Up.

Muswell Hill. The sitting room is empty. There is the sound of the front door closing, left, then PETER *enters. He has had a monstrous hair-cut, is neatly and newly suited. He is carrying flowers and chocolates. He stands staring, then hears noises in the kitchen. Moves towards it.* CHARLES *emerges. He is eating a carrot.*

There is a long pause.

PETER. Well Charlie, I'm back. Where's Hilary?

CHARLES. Gone to have a bath.

PETER. Ah! What are you doing here?

CHARLES. I came to collect the pot. I was just leaving.

There is a pause.

CHARLES. And how's your girl?

PETER. Did you mention her to Hilary?

CHARLES. No.

PETER. Thank you.

CHARLES. For Hilary's sake, not yours.

PETER. Naturally. *(Looks towards the door, then at* CHARLES*).* Oh for God's sake don't look so censorious. My tail is back between my legs, where it belongs. Isn't that what you wanted?

CHARLES. But should you be smirking?

PETER. Am I? Well, it's a family trait in moments of embarrassment. As you should know.

CHARLES. Embarrassment? Is that what you call this mess? You walk out on your wife and son after weeks of the most repellent behaviour, all for the sake of some heartless little creature—and then you turn up with a hair cut and in a new suit and refer smirkingly to embarrassment. Well let me tell *you*—

PETER. No, please don't, Charlie. Please don't tell me anything. I know.

CHARLES. *(biting angrily at the carrot).* *What* do you know?

PETER. Well, for one thing, I know that you couldn't just go off, could you, and have a casual affair with some heartless creature, just like that, after weeks of the most repellent behaviour. Could you?

CHARLES. No, I damn well could not!

PETER. Well nor could I. *(Sinks into the chair).* I could manage the repellent behaviour, but not the heartless creature.

CHARLES. You mean nothing happened?

PETER. Nothing to speak of. Although I expect she'll speak of it, all right.

CHARLES. So you haven't betrayed Hilary after all?

PETER. Oh yes. I betrayed them both, given their different expectations. But incompetently. Neither a successful adulterer nor a faithful husband. Something between the two.

CHARLES. I did warn you that you couldn't go back.

PETER. To what?

CHARLES. To your old promiscuity. Your Gertas, your Friedas, your—*(Gesture)*.

PETER. My André Gide's daughters. *(Laughs)*.

CHARLES. Oh, I've remembered since. It was Cocteau's daughter.

PETER. You can't honestly believe Cocteau had a daughter either?

CHARLES. I don't honestly care whose daughter it was. Whose was it anyway?

PETER. Cocteau's.

CHARLES. You just said he didn't have a daughter.

PETER. Exactly.

CHARLES. *(after a long pause, tensely)*. What do you mean?

PETER. Isn't it perfectly obvious?

CHARLES. There isn't any famous French writer's daughter?

PETER. I'm sure there are lots. But I've never slept with them.

CHARLES. And the Gertas, the Friedas, the Italian painters, the ballet dancer who was old enough to be your mother.

PETER. I think it was the Italian painter who was old enough to be my mother. Unless it was a retired ballet dancer. Or Margot Fonteyn.

CHARLES. You made them all up?

PETER. *We* made them all up, really, Charlie. The two of us. Your indignation gave substance to my fantasies. Without your help they'd never have existed for me—

and they seem to have gone on existing for you. They died for me years ago, isn't that funny.

CHARLES. So Hilary was the first girl you went all the way with.

PETER. The only anything I've ever been all the way with, except of course for that old sock.

CHARLES. *(sits staring ahead)*. You lied to me, all these years.

PETER. No. I lied to you years ago, and you've just gone on believing it all these years.

CHARLES. Why did you lie to me *then* then?

PETER. You seemed to expect that sort of thing from me. It seemed a shame to go on letting you down. Besides, you were so righteously convinced that I wasn't at all like you, it helped me to believe the same thing. I knew that we were both sheep, but my seeming a black one added a bit of colour to our joint self. *(Pause)*. But aren't you glad that underneath we're *both* such decent chaps. I've never done anything of which you'd *really* disapprove—at least not until after I left Hilary and even that—well, here I am after all.

CHARLES. We're not the same. We're not!

PETER. In what are we different then, except in Alison's fecundity. And I've frequently *longed* for more children. It's Hilary who's against that—since she started going back to work.

CHARLES. Well—well—you and Hilary, you made love long before you were married. Before you were engaged, even. Or was *that* a lie too?

PETER. Not quite. The first time we went to bed we didn't manage to get quite all the way. The second

76

time we weren't engaged for most of the way, but we were by the time we'd gone all of it. It was a package deal. She insisted.

CHARLES. On your getting engaged?

PETER. On my going all the way. Getting engaged was my solution for getting there. Brothers Charlie, you see, under the skin. *(Gets up, shows his hands to CHARLIE)*. What do you see?

CHARLES. Your hands? *(Studies them)*. Nicotine stains, otherwise—*(Shakes his head)* just your hands.

PETER. Not mine any longer. Daddy's. I never noticed them while he was alive but I recognise them now he's dead. Living heirlooms, without the liver spots. Doubtless they'll come.

CHARLES looks at his own hands.

You have Mummy's hands, to the very cuticle. As you don't smoke either. The rest of us is, of course, the usual hodge-podge of inherited characteristics, some too far back to be traceable. I wonder whose hands Jeremy will recognise when he gets to our age . . . *(Pause)*. Anyway, we're on our way, you and I.

CHARLES. On our way where?

PETER. Just on. And on. Through these early middle into the late middle, the late late middle or the early late—and so on and on, until pegging out. If not before. Somebody's father, somebody's husband, somebody's editor in my case, some Headmaster's Assistant in yours, somebody's brother in both our cases, eh Charlie? All relationships and no self. Not even our own hands.

CHARLES. So you attribute my—our—being faithful husbands to genetics, do you? What balderdash.

PETER. I'm not attributing it to anything, I'm merely saying that we are. It could be inherited. Daddy's mousiness, Mummy's prohibitiveness, it could be sweet-rationing.

CHARLES. Sweet-rationing?

PETER. Well, we did catch the last few years of it, remember, in our sweet-eating prime. Perhaps ration coupons for chocolates conditioned us to marriage licences for sex. I don't know.

CHARLES. And all those friends of yours that you cited —with their affairs and divorces.

PETER. I don't know. Perhaps their parents were on the black-market. Perhaps they were just unlucky. Or lucky. I don't know. But I'll tell you something, every break-up shocked me as much as it would have shocked you. *(Pause).* Hilary knew I'd come back to her, Charlie, all the time. She knows me.

CHARLES. But why should she take you back?

PETER. Well, for one thing, if I'm to be monogamous male, I'll need my only wife. *(Pause).* But aren't you pleased that I'm a shining reflection of your own virtue: you don't seem to be. I don't expect much rejoicing in Heaven for the sheep back in the fold, as I've scarcely left it, but I thought you'd be—well, at the very least *satisfied*.

CHARLES. *(after a pause).* But we're not the same in our attitudes to our work, are we?

PETER. I've been a most conscientious editor. Furthermore I like my job, on the whole.

CHARLES. But the way you've always sneered at my getting ahead. Virtually accused me of *ingratiating* myself—

PETER. Now there it's true I always thought there was a difference, I did despise some of your ploys. But not any more, Charlie. I've since found out that in a crisis we're identical there, too.

CHARLIE. Identical in what?

PETER. At that party—the six simultaneous publications party—I made some remarks. At the top of my voice. Which I subsequently regretted. Actually, I regretted them a second before I made them.

CHARLES. Then why did you make them?

PETER. So as not to waste the regret. Anyway, my job hung in the balance, and I thought, as I set out to save it, that if you could do it with Headmaster and wife, I could do it with my lot.

CHARLES. Do what?

PETER. Grovel. With telegrams at first—I thought I might get a cheap deal with the post office. Apology cables on the lines of Greetings Cables. But I had to stop after the first two, I couldn't bear the operator's tone as he read them back to me. In the end I used taxis and grovelled direct. It was surprisingly easy.

CHARLES. *(goes over to the drinks table)*. You found it so, did you?

PETER. By drawing on your example. I pretended I was you and whomever I was grovelling to was either Headmaster, if a woman, or Headmaster's wife, if a man. In no time at all I was doing it *in propria persona*. And all these years I've sneered at you for practising what I was ashamed to realise in myself. So you see, Charlie, there's a good chance that we'll make it to the top together, just as Mummy would have wished, on all fours so to speak, and side by side. As you consult with

Eton's Provost over your next raise or domicile, you'll be able to think of my fawning figure closing in on a Directorship in publishing.

CHARLIE. Did you know you were out of soda water?

PETER. Then I shall order some more. Nuzek was so taken with my performance that he actually asked me to repeat it tomorrow, over lunch. At which I'll gobble down humble-pie with relish. *(Pause).* Now I'd better go up and do some grovelling to my wife, eh? *(Looks at CHARLES).* Charlie, what *is* it ? You don't look yourself, and I've given you such a chance to be, only more so. You've skimped dreadfully on the I-told-you-sos. Haven't I earned them? *(Pause).* Is everything all right at home? *(Pause).* Alison all right? The kids?

CHARLES. Fine. Fine.

PETER. *(hesitates, then brightly).* By the way, something occurred to me about that dog.

CHARLES. Dog?

PETER. Dog. Your adopted dog. Alfonso wasn't it— Hadn't you better make sure that Headmaster really doesn't mind him hanging about the garden before feeding him? Some people hate strays—

CHARLES leaps across the room, seizes PETER by the lapels, shakes him vigorously.

Hey—Hey—

CHARLES lets him go.

Christ, what was *that* for? Haven't I grovelled enough, even for you.

CHARLES. *(hits him on the upper arm, sharply and spitefully).* You little—

80

PETER. Ow, you sod!

CHARLES. Bastard! *(Turns, walks off, stage left. Sound of front door slamming).*

PETER. Christ! *(Rubs his arm, after a minute gets up, goes to the drinks table, picks up the scotch bottle, after a short struggle with himself puts it down. Hesitates, then goes across to the flowers and chocolates. Picks them up. Turns to the door, left).*

HILARY enters in a bathrobe. Looks at PETER.

PETER. *(turns. After a moment)* Good evening.

HILARY. Charlie left then?

PETER. Well, first he shook me half senseless, clouted me on the arm, and called me little bastard. Then he left. What was interesting is that he chose the place where he used to get me, day in and day out, up to fifteen years ago. It's soft and painful, doesn't do permanent damage, and leaves no bruise for a parental eye.

HILARY. Were you baiting him?

PETER. On the contrary. I was simply pointing out that we were brothers under the skin, and offering him some practical advice. Perhaps that's it—now I've shown him how my life has run, I've released all his sibling rivalry. *(Laughs nervously. There is a pause).* Anyway I've come—*(hesitates)* home. Groomed for the occasion. What do you think of my hair-cut, by the way? Executed by a great traditionalist in Holborn. He was so delighted to get back to old-fashioned hair-shearing that he tried to do it for nothing. I had to insist. *(Pause).* But I didn't charge him much. *(Laughs).* Well, the last time we spoke, you seemed to be hankering for what I'd once been. No other part of me is so immediately susceptible to backwards change. And look—*(Holds out chocolates and flowers)* more *memorabilia* from our wooing past.

HILARY makes no move.

Am I smirking?

HILARY. Not noticeably.

PETER. Oh, well I ought to be. I'm very embarrassed. Not to say frightened even. *(Little pause)*. Surely you *knew* I'd come back.

HILARY. Yes.

PETER. And that I'd apologise for—well, you know.

HILARY. Yes.

PETER. Well—*(Puts the flowers and chocolates on the table)*. How's Jeremy?

HILARY. He's asleep.

PETER. Oh good. And how's school? His, I mean?

HILARY. All right.

PETER. Still not reading, I suppose?

HILARY. Since the weekend he's moved on to the second *Janet and John*.

PETER. Let's hope the narrative is beginning to gather pace. And how are you?

HILARY. Perfectly well, thank you.

PETER. Look Hil, I've missed you and him and everything—perhaps it was worth my going to find *that* out—not that I didn't know it. But now the fact of it makes me happy, as it did when we first lived together. *(Pause)*. I know the fault was mine, *entirely* mine. I was taking my frustrations out on you and was being altogether childish. I had no right to do it, no right to walk out— *(This very quickly)*.

HILARY. But I asked you to.

PETER. Well, I made it impossible for you not to, didn't I? A fairly familiar marital ploy, I expect, so that when one gets tired of playing the role of culprit one can have a go at being the victim. Well, I shan't do *that* anyway. I abjectly admit that it was all *my* doing.

HILARY. No it wasn't.

PETER. Oh yes it was Hil, I drove you past the point of tolerance, I know that. But now what I desperately want is to put it behind us, with the understanding of course that you can put it in front of me during any healthy little marital spat of the future. *(Smiles)*. I've brought you something else, by the way. *(Takes a sheet of paper out of his pocket, hands it to HILARY)*. The first items I've already made a start of putting into effect—the haircut is, I admit, a little excessive, but at least it takes care of the dandruff, for which there's no longer any room. I've also gargled my throat raw, my present huskiness isn't all emotion, you know, and as for items two and three, I haven't smoked since three this afternoon, and the scotch I needed before facing you I didn't actually swallow. Now you'll see that I've been able to give a firm commitment on Sainsbury's for Saturday mornings but that any evening treks would, of course, be subject to various career responsibilities. *(Little pause)*. Both our careers, that is. I admit that the way I've shared the business of taking Jeremy to school seems a trifle inequitable on a quick glance, but then I had to take into account that you drive and I don't. Three mornings for you and two for me therefore seems reasonable, but I am, you'll note, prepared to re-negotiate as particular weeks make particular demands. *(Pause)*. The clause on sex at the end was, of course, the trickiest and required several draftings but you'll see that the only emphatic stipulation is a shared bed. The declaration with which I precede my signature is true. Where it says I love you and always will. *(Pause)*. I've kept a second copy for myself as a *memento mori*—I mean, *aide memoire*, but I thought of doing a third and circulating it to the registry office. They may feel it's worth incorporating into the current exchange of vows. Thus bridegrooms could make an immediate start on inflating into husbands. Of eight years standing.

HILARY finishes reading the paper.

You don't seem very interested. Have I left something out?

HILARY. Nothing really.

PETER. But don't you want me to make a fresh start?

HILARY. But we're not very fresh any more, Pete. Either of us.

PETER. Well, what about an advance then, from where we used to be at our best? *(Pause)*. Hil—I'm not asking you for anything except the most precious thing in the world for me. To say that it's all right really.

HILARY. But it isn't.

PETER. But surely you *can* say—well, you know. That you love me, and always will, whatever.

HILARY. That's for children, not grown-ups.

PETER. *(after a pause)*. That's Jeremy taken care of. At least for your life-time, as he'll go on being your child, to the day he—*(Stops)*. And mine too. Ours. *(Pause, takes a step forward)*. Oh Hil—*(steps towards her)*.

HILARY. Don't! *(Crying out)*.

PETER. *(stops)*. Because—just because—Charlie has been talking, has he?

HILARY. Almost non-stop. But not about you.

PETER. But then what is it? I mean, all right, all right, I've conceded that I deserve punishing—

HILARY. That's for children too.

PETER. Surely not these days. I thought that was why adults had to settle for punishing each other. *(Pause)*. All right, let me put it another way. I'm back in my own maisonette, what are you going to do about it?

HILARY. Ask you to leave.

PETER. Are you going to explain, or just go on being ruthlessly gnomic?

HILARY. I'm trying to avoid an ugly scene.

PETER. This is your idea of a pretty one, is it?

HILARY. Would you please leave, Peter. I'll tell you everything in a letter.

PETER. In a letter! *(Incredulously)*. A letter! Well darling, I promise you I shall receive it at my own front door. Because I'm bloody not going. I've discovered I'm too young to leave home. I'm sticking, upstairs, downstairs, in the kitchen, in your way, I'm your husband, Jeremy's father. And what are you going to do about that? Call in the lawyers and the policemen?

HILARY. If I have to. *(Pause)*. Anyway, now you know

I really want you to go, and that I shall go on wanting you to go. And until you do—you stay down here. I'm going to bed.

PETER. No, you're not. *(Takes her arm).* Do you really think you can get out of it after eight years of my love *and* devotion because I've given you a few bad times recently? Well, what about my bad times, the ones I can't escape from though I've just tried—and I'm not talking about your neglect of me for your work, your increasing frigidity and those calculated little aloofnesses that *you* started practising even before I started practising going to seed.

HILARY. Is that why you did it? So that I'd take a little notice of you?

PETER. I'm talking about the real bad times, the ones that have come every day of my life since I first began to love you. When the telephone rings in my office and before I answer it I think of you in a car crash or of Jeremy ill or maimed in some idiotic accident at school—or the sudden hopeless questions, such as 'But what should I do if anything happened to either of you?' as I know it's bound to, to both of you in the end, and that all I can really pray for is that it happens to me first, after a decent interval, and then that there are further decent intervals between your going and his. Except that life doesn't work according to decent intervals, which are anyway formulated by types like you and me out here in Muswell Hill.

HILARY. Shut up, shut up, this isn't fair.

PETER. Precisely my point. But it's true.

HILARY. Of course it's true. Do you think I haven't thought the same about Jeremy.

PETER. But not about me?

HILARY. Yes. But it doesn't matter.

PETER. Doesn't matter!

HILARY. Because I'm still going to live my own life. *(Pause)*. Oh God, Peter, it's not the beginning, when we were in love with each other. Or the end, when we could have cried over each other, and probably still will, both those parts are easy, anyone can do those. It's the stretch in between, that's our married life, that I can't stand.

PETER. Because for a short time, a matter of months, what, three months—

HILARY. Oh longer. Much longer.

PETER. Four then, at the most. Before that, I was a model husband, father, the lot! Second only to Charlie.

HILARY. I wouldn't want to be married to Charlie either. But he's found himself an Alison, why couldn't you?

PETER. What!

HILARY. Did you sleep with anyone, while you were away?

PETER. Is that what you think?

HILARY. Well, did you?

PETER. I certainly did not!

HILARY. Why not?

PETER. Because I couldn't—it's not in my nature— perhaps I tried, I won't deny it—we went to bed together, yes, all right—but we didn't make love! *You* know I couldn't!

HILARY. Why not?

PETER. You wouldn't let me! When it came to it I didn't want a foreign body next to mine in bed, and that's the truth. I felt clumsy and awkward and dirty, and that's the truth too. So you can't make anything out of that Hilary. I may not be so in law, but *you* know I'm a faithful husband.

HILARY. Yes, I know. And that's what I can't stand.

PETER. What?

HILARY. Pete—you're married to a faithless wife.

PETER. What?

HILARY. Oh why didn't you come back as you left—drunken and sneering. You look so—so *clean!*

PETER. You mean there's somebody else?

HILARY nods.

In ten days you found a replacement—well, send him back. *(Goes and sits down).*

HILARY. Not in ten days. A long time ago! I *wanted* you to go, I *wanted* you to go, I wanted you to *go.* I couldn't bear your wretched innocence, your oppressive faithfulness. It's been like deceiving a child.

PETER. It's not—*(Blankly, after a second)* fair. At that bloody school of yours, is he?

HILARY. Yes.

PETER. Well what is he—some damned—foreigner? What? A Turk, an Arab, a Spanish monk, a Frenchman—how low *have* you sunk?

HILARY. He's a teacher.

PETER. To the very bottom then! What's his name?

HILARY. What does it matter?

PETER. *What's his name!*

HILARY. Please, you'll wake Jeremy. George Green.

PETER. George Green. You've never mentioned any George Green. Nothing. Nothing. No passing references to any George Green, no murmurings in your sleep of George Green, no smiling by-the-ways-have-I-told-you-about-George-Green. Nothing. I don't believe it.

HILARY. It's true, Peter. I love him.

PETER. Love George Green! Well, come on, come on, what is he? Married, widowed, divorced, one of these fashionably converting homosexuals, he can't be single unless he's a mere boy, is he a mere boy, George Green?

HILARY. No. He's older than us, actually.

PETER. How much older?

HILARY. By ten years.

PETER. Divorced, eh? How many times?

HILARY. Twice.

PETER. A bit of a specialist then, but not versatile. Or has he just been practising until the right married woman, my wife, came along? How many children?

HILARY. Two by his first wife, one by his second.

PETER. But is he trained in children over five? Or does he pass them on at an early age? I'm speaking for Jeremy now.

HILARY. He sees a great deal of them.

PETER. And he sees a great deal of mine?

HILARY. Not yet. *(Pause)*. Peter, I—

PETER. Shut up!

HILARY. *(after a pause)*. I didn't set out to look for another man. I really didn't. It happened because, well, I didn't believe you'd go on being faithful.

PETER laughs.

HILARY. Well, nobody else has! You and Charlie are quite extraordinary, you see. After I'd gone back to work I suddenly realised that when I'm menopausal you'll be in your sexy forties, and in our fifties you'd be all right if you watched your eating and drinking, but I'd be a woman in my fifties, you see. And in our sixties you could be having it off with girls in their twenties even. I may feel a woman in my sixties, but to most men, including you, I'd be just a woman in my sixties, with almost certainly a hysterectomy—when God knows, I'd be struggling for the pride not to check your pockets or your underwear drawer before doing both, probably. *(Pause)*. So that when George showed he was interested in me at least I knew I was still desirable. I never meant it to turn serious.

PETER. It had no other way to turn, from such a beginning. And does he want to marry you?

HILARY. Yes.

PETER. And you him?

HILARY. I think so, yes. Anyway, I want you to move out straight away.

PETER. Oh, but just a minute darling, isn't it slightly unconventional to see me from our bedroom to the drawing-room sofa to the side-walk, back again and out again, all within ten days. Most marriages conclude at a slightly more leisurely pace—we're skimping on the niceties—we've been complacent witnesses to a lot of break-ups in our time, we must owe returns to newly re-weds and divorcees all over London. For God's sake let's stick to form, by your own admission

we haven't even begun to make Jeremy miserable—
what about the heart-searchings followed by the
heart-rendings, yours and mine—*(Stops, gestures
futilely)*.

HILARY. But why did you think, why, that our marriage
was going to survive. Nobody else's has, that we know.
Except for Jeff and Davina Wainwright's, and isn't it
better to end up apart than together like them?
(Pause). If only you'd been unfaithful I might have
managed it—but you've always assumed I was to be
your full-time wife, even when you began to resent me,
as recently. When I became your full-time resentment.
Your dependence fills me with a guilt I can't bear, life's
too short . . . Don't you see . . . *(Coming over, puts
her hand on his head)*.

PETER. Don't do that! *(Sharply, then)*. They still stock
period Brylcream in Holborn, my period anyway.
(Pause). Go to bed, Hilary, leave me alone.

HILARY hesitates, then turns, goes to the door, left.

After all you'll have another of your hard days
tomorrow won't you, with all its explanations, caresses,
half-plans, avowals and pronunciation classes not to
speak of collecting Jeremy from school, then buying
me a Chinese throw-away *and* facing me over it—.

HILARY goes out.

*PETER reaches for a cigarette, takes out the package,
studies it, then turns it on its side, studies the Govern-
ment Warning, reads it carefully, then takes out a
cigarette, lights it. Sits staring ahead.
There is a crashing noise from the kitchen. PETER looks
towards the kitchen.*

CHARLES. *(enters. He is carrying a syphon of soda water).* I got you some. *(Holds up the syphon).*

PETER. Thanks.

CHARLES. Well, I do drink so much of it—*(Carries it across to the table, puts it down).* Um, may I—?

PETER. Help yourself.

CHARLES. *(squirts some into a glass).* I'm sorry about before. Drink?

PETER. Please.

CHARLES. *(pours him a very small scotch, brings it over).* That's the first time in twenty years I've hit you.

PETER. *(looking at the scotch in dismay).* At least it was evocative.

CHARLES. No hard feelings.

PETER. No. But I don't know why you did it.

CHARLES. Nor do I really. *(Pause).* By the way, I don't know if Hilary told you, we're going to have twins.

PETER. You and Hilary?

CHARLES. *(laughs).* Alison is, I should say.

PETER. Twins, Charlie. Congratulations.

CHARLES. Thanks. *(Little pause).* Is everything all right between you two?

PETER. Oh yes.

CHARLES. Well, you said it would be. You told her everything, did you?

PETER. I think we're much clearer about each other, Charlie, thanks.

CHARLES. Even about that girl eh, and going to bed with her, even though—.

PETER. She knows everything, even about Cocteau's daughter.

CHARLES. But I realised afterwards that she'd never known about her. Them. I mean, how could you tell her about affairs you never had?

PETER. I didn't have to tell her, she always knew I didn't have them. After all, she virtually had to give me directions on our engagement night.

CHARLES. She's very understanding. *(Little pause).* You know, I'm sorry they didn't exist.

PETER. So am I. So, probably, is she. But then I'd have been a different sort of person and—

CHARLES. And she wouldn't have wanted to marry you.

PETER. Yes. A bit of a conundrum, that.

CHARLES. And she does love you. That's one thing Alison and I have never doubted, through all this. Now that you've confessed your self, which is real, after all, isn't it? Rather than your sins, which weren't— That's too metaphysical for me. Still, Alison's always said I'm more Catholic than she is by nature, so probably you are too. *(Long pause, laughs).* Remember how I confessed to Mummy that I'd almost stolen some of those Laura Secord Chocolates Aunt Mabel sent from Canada during the war.

PETER. But only to draw attention to the fact that I'd actually stolen them. Didn't Mummy give you three of them as a reward? Not really confessing, Charlie, more a sordid combination of sneaking and scrounging.

CHARLES. That's a lie! I didn't know you had! *(Pause).* Oh Heavens, yes I did. You're quite right. I admit it. *(Laughs).*

PETER smiles.

Anyway, I'm glad you're back, Pete. I missed you. I mean, the great thing is, isn't it, to love one another in spite.

PETER. In spite? Yes, I'll drink to that. *(Raises his glass).*

CHARLES. *(raises his).* In spite. *(Then very emotionally).* Welcome home, Pete.

PETER. Thank you.

PETER and CHARLES drink.

CHARLES. Well, *(Gets up)* I'd better be going, Alison will worry. *(Turns to the door, right).* Old Pete.

PETER. Old Charlie. *(Also emotionally. Gets up).*

CHARLES. *(exits, holding his glass).* Ooops! *(Crashing sound).*

PETER holding his glass, smiles. Picks up flowers and chocolates, follows CHARLES into the kitchen.

PETER. *(from the kitchen).* For Alison. And the twins.

CHARLES. *(from the kitchen).* Are you sure, but what about Hilary?

PETER. *(from the kitchen).* She's very fond—she'll be pleased.

CHARLES. *(from the kitchen).* So will Alison. She's very fond too.

The room, as they speak, fills with sunlight.

JOANNA after a moment enters. She is carrying a mug.

PETER. *(from kitchen).* Don't think of it as coffee, but as a quite other drink. Then try to like the other drink, and you're home.

JOANNA. *(sips).* It's great. *(Looks vaguely at the photograph).*

PETER enters. Hair slightly longer.

I'm glad you like my covers, that really means a lot to me.

PETER. I hope you're going to do lots for me.

There is a pause. PETER comes over, takes the mug from her. Puts it down.

This can wait.

JOANNA. What for?

PETER goes over to the sofa, begins to slip off the sofa mattress.

I thought you said you had to see somebody at your office this afternoon.

PETER. Oh, he can wait, too.

JOANNA. I hope it's not a poet. I couldn't bear to keep a poet waiting.

PETER. I'm first, you can get around to him later. Zealander. *(Little pause).* Anyway, I'm first, you can get around to him later.

JOANNA. What if that landlady of yours comes back?

PETER. On a Wednesday? *(Goes over to JOANNA, kisses her).* It's her Sainsbury evening.

JOANNA. She's not your landlady, she's your wife, isn't she? You're married, aren't you?

PETER. *(after a pause).* Am I?

Lights

CURTAIN